pedaling tandem for the long haul

REALLIFESTUFFFORCOUPLES ON **MANAGING YOUR MARRIAGE**

A NavStudy Featuring *The* **MESSAGE**®

Written and compiled by Tim McLaughlin

NAVPRESS®

BRINGING TRUTH TO LIFE

OUR GUARANTEE TO YOU

We believe so strongly in the message of our books that we are making this quality guarantee to you. If for any reason you are disappointed with the content of this book, return the title page to us with your name and address and we will refund to you the list price of the book. To help us serve you better, please briefly describe why you were disappointed. Mail your refund request to: NavPress, P.O. Box 35002, Colorado Springs, CO 80935.

The Navigators is an international Christian organization. Our mission is to advance the gospel of Jesus and His kingdom into the nations through spiritual generations of laborers living and discipling among the lost. We see a vital movement of the gospel, fueled by prevailing prayer, flowing freely through relational networks and out into the nations where workers for the kingdom are next door to everywhere.

NavPress is the publishing ministry of The Navigators. The mission of NavPress is to reach, disciple, and equip people to know Christ and make Him known by publishing life-related materials that are biblically rooted and culturally relevant. Our vision is to stimulate spiritual transformation through every product we publish.

ISBN-10: 1-60006-163-X
ISBN-13: 978-1-60006-163-9

Cover design by Chris Gilbert/Studio Gearbox/www.studiogearbox.com
Cover image by Getty
Creative Team: Terry Behimer, John Blase, Cara Iverson, Darla Hightower, Arvid Wallen, Kathy Guist

Written and compiled by Tim McLaughlin

Some of the anecdotal illustrations in this book are true to life and are included with the permission of the persons involved. All other illustrations are composites of real situations, and any resemblance to people living or dead is coincidental.

Unless otherwise identified, all Scripture quotations in this publication are taken from *THE MESSAGE* (MSG). Copyright © 1993, 1994, 1995, 1996, 2000, 2001, 2002. Used by permission of NavPress Publishing Group.

Printed in the United States of America

1 2 3 4 5 6 / 11 10 09 08 07

FOR A FREE CATALOG OF NAVPRESS BOOKS & BIBLE STUDIES,
CALL 1-800-366-7788 (USA) OR 1-800-839-4769 (CANADA).

contents

about the
REALLIFESTUFFFORCOUPLES
series

Let your love dictate how you deal with me;
    teach me from your textbook on life.
I'm your servant—help me understand what that means,
    the inner meaning of your instructions. . . .
Break open your words, let the light shine out,
    let ordinary people see the meaning.

Psalm 119:124-125,130

We're all yearning for understanding, for truth, wisdom, hope. Whether
we quietly simmer in uncertainty or boil over into blatant unbelief, we
long for a better life, a more meaningful existence, a more fulfilling marriage. We want our marriages to matter—to ourselves most of all, and
then to our children and the rest of our families and friends. But real-life
stuff—the urgency of daily life with all its responsibilities, major and minor
catastrophes, conversations, dreams, and all—tends to fog up the image
of the marriage we crave. And so we go on with the way things are.

    We can pretend that there's really no problem, that everything is
actually fine, thank you. We can intensify the same old way we've been
living, hoping that more is better. We can flee—emotionally, spiritually,
literally.

Whether or not we face it head-on, real life matters. In that fog there are things about ourselves, our spouses, and our marriages that cause distress, discomfort, and dis-ease.

The REAL LIFE STUFF FOR COUPLES series is a safe place for exploring the truth about that fog. It's not your typical Bible study—no fill-in-the-blank questions, no one telling you what things mean or what to do. In fact, you'll probably finish a REAL LIFE STUFF study with more questions than you started with. But through personal reflection and lively conversation in your small group (you know this is the best part of a Bible study anyway), these books will take you where you need to go—and in the process bring greater hope and meaning to your life.

Each REAL LIFE STUFF FOR COUPLES book gives you the space to ask the hard questions about marriage—yours and others'. A space to find comfort in the chaos. A space to enlarge your understanding of your marriage, your God, and where those two intersect.

And—with the guidance of the Holy Spirit—a space to discover real-life hope for your marriage that brings meaning to the everyday challenge of crafting a life together.

introduction

These days, marriage is an emotional contract, a deal. There are as many kinds of deals as there are marriages. When the deal changes, with the birth of a child, with the loss of a job or a parent, or with the inevitable alterations of age, both parties have to adjust to the new deal. Those who take the attitude that a deal is a deal will probably not be able to stay married. Life isn't real estate.

—SUSAN CHEEVER, IN HER ESSAY "MRS. MARRIED PERSON," IN
WHY I'M STILL MARRIED: WOMEN WRITE THEIR HEARTS OUT ON LOVE, LOSS, SEX,
AND WHO DOES THE DISHES

Put GOD in charge of your work, then what you've planned will take place.

—PROVERBS 16:3

It pays to take life seriously; things work out when you trust in GOD.

—PROVERBS 16:20

Marriage, American style: a fusion of civil contract, property transfer, and lifelong romance.

A forced fusion, some say, that cannot hold up under its own rosy expectations. After all, society has only recently expected marriage and romance to coexist (with the same person) for any length of time. Which probably explains the miles of bookshelves of self-help volumes on marriage, relationships, communication, making your spouse your soul mate, nurturing your marriage, healing it, strengthening it, enlivening it.

Those millions of pages of advice are testament to the stark and quite unromantic truth that a contractual relationship can tootle along indefinitely, with or without talking to each other, confiding in each other, indulging in each other. While marriage as a contractual agreement can coast until deliberately nullified, romance must be continually reinvigorated, recharged, refueled, exercised, coached, and coddled if it is to endure in some form out to ten, twenty, fifty years. And if halfway through the lifetime of a marriage romance is gradually replaced by comfortable companionship, some say (many by experience) that that will do too.

Among the many metaphors for marriage, the language of progressive local government is surprisingly apropos. Consider these phrases, which actually describe an American city's process of change: "visioning the future . . . think big about what we value most . . . what changes in the demographics we'll need to be planning for in the future . . . what changes we'll want to initiate . . . stakeholders owning the process . . . address the most pressing issues facing our community."

These words could as well describe a purposeful marriage. Your marriage is no less a community, albeit a community of two. It is a community whose demographics change as children are born into and grow out of it. Your own marital community cherishes certain values, whether or not those values are debated, celebrated, tacitly accepted, or ignored. The two of you are the stakeholders in your community—whatever happens within your marriage, whether by proactive decision making by you or by outside influence (other people, other forces), you and your spouse are the ones who live with the results.

This is intentionality. Being deliberate in your marriage, planning with purpose, deciding what direction to take your marital partnership—career directions, lifestyle directions, domestic directions. Directions of sex, finances, child rearing, family rearing.

Intentionality, deliberateness, purposefulness—these all connote forward-thinking, a vision reaching further than merely next week or even next year, paying attention less to quarterly reports and more to what you want to see a decade from now. Let's return to the urban-planning motif for a moment: What would happen if you and your spouse approached a long view of your marriage like a handful of Seattleites recently approached the long view of their city? To protect their Northwest quality of life for their great-grandchildren a hundred years from now, the group put their heads together and did what "doesn't really happen in America anymore," in the words of a former mayor of Seattle and a member of the group. "Corporate America plans for its new quarterly reports, government plans as far as the next election—so it was a real thrill to sit down with a bunch of smart people . . . and elevate the conversation to a higher level." To the year 2100, to be exact.

Sometimes taking the long view means veering out of the current of prevailing wisdom, even swimming against the current, standing against active opposition. Just a few hours down Interstate 5 from Seattle is Portland, Oregon, where—back in the 1950s and '60s—the city fathers proposed a Los Angeles–type freeway system that (among other things) would have eviscerated thriving urban neighborhoods. A citizen opposition organized and eventually killed the proposal, in the process diverting the millions of federal transportation dollars originally earmarked for freeways to a light-rail system instead. Many one-person-per-car suburban commuters, stuck in heavy traffic on the region's few freeways, still curse the decision.

Yet Portland's light-rail, now twenty years old, is delivering on its then visionary promise: It now carries more than a quarter of all rush-hour commuters along the main commuting routes. And you don't need a calculator to imagine the fuel saved (millions of gallons a year) and air pollutants avoided (tons a day). Granted, it cost a few more dollars to build a light-rail system than to add lanes to freeways or more bus routes—but then, the city was thinking twenty and fifty years and more down the road, not just getting the most bang for their buck at the moment.

For Portland's transportation department, the long view meant deliberately and courageously planning for a day that most could not imagine in the late '60s: scarce and prohibitively expensive oil, yet also a city whose urban qualities made it a place where people actually wanted to live and work instead of flee.

For you and your spouse, the long view may mean deliberately and courageously planning for—well, here's where you decide what it is you want. Children, no children, more children, or a cap on your family size? Expand to a two-income household, or downsize to one income? Will you live an urban, suburban, or rural lifestyle—and are you aware of and willing to live with the dark sides of those lifestyles? Buy or rent? Make do with one car, a bicycle or two, and public transportation—or a car for each of you? What will be the role in your family of TV? Of travel? To what degree will you schedule your life around children? Around aging parents? Around your spouse's job instead of your own? Feeling like it's time to change churches? If so, what makes you feel so?

If the two of you happen to agree on most of these points, good for you—enjoy it while it lasts, make hay while the sun shines, strike while the iron's hot. That is, such concord seldom lasts long, not to mention a lifetime. You will change, your spouse will change, your circumstances will change—and when most people pause and think, they realize they'd not have it any other way. There will be—there should be—negotiations, compromises, diplomatic exchanges of the domestic sort, gracious listening, tactful propositions, theorizing, envisioning, dreaming.

For this is what it looks like, what it feels like, to be deliberate in your primary relationship—to have an intentional marriage.

how to
use this
discussion guide

This discussion guide is meant to be completed by you and your spouse—*and* in a small group of married couples. So before you dive into this book, put together a discussion group. Maybe the two of you already belong to a couples' group. That works just fine. Or maybe you know three or four couples who could do coffee once a week. That works, too. Ask around. You'll be surprised how many of your coworkers, teammates, or neighbors would be interested in a small-group study, especially a study like this that doesn't require vast biblical knowledge. A group of three or four couples is optimal—any bigger and one or more members will likely be shut out of discussions. Or your small group can be only you two and another couple. Choose a couple who's not afraid to talk with you honestly and authentically about themselves. Make sure all participants have their own copies of this book.

1. *Read* the Bible passages and other readings in each lesson as a couple or on your own. Let it all soak in. Then use the white space provided to "think out loud on paper." Note content in the readings that troubles you, inspires you, confuses you, or challenges you. Be honest. Be bold. Don't shy away from the hard things. If you don't understand the passage, say so to your spouse, to your group. If you don't agree, say that, too. You may choose to cover a lesson in one thirty- to forty-five-minute focused session. Or perhaps you'll spend twenty minutes a day on the readings.

2. *Think* about what you read. Think about what you wrote. Always ask, "What does this mean?" and "Why does this matter?" about the readings. Compare different Bible translations. Respond to the questions we've provided. You may have a lot to say on one topic, little on another. Allow the experience of others to broaden your experience. You'll be stretched here—called upon to evaluate what you've discovered and asked to make practical sense of it. In a group, that stretching can often be painful and sometimes embarrassing. But your willingness to be transparent—your openness to the possibility of personal growth—will reap great rewards.

3. *Pray* as you go through the entire session: before you read a word, in the middle of your thinking process, when you get stuck on a concept or passage, and as you approach the time when you'll explore these passages and thoughts together in a small group. Pray with your spouse, pray by yourself. Pray for inspiration, pray in frustration. Speak your prayers, write your prayers in this book, or let your silence be a prayer.

4. *Live.* (That's "live" as in rhymes with "give" as in "Give me something that will benefit my marriage.") Before you and your spouse meet with your small group, complete as much of this section as you can (particularly the "What I Want to Discuss" section). Then, in your small group, ask the hard questions about what the lesson means to you. (You know, the questions everyone is thinking, but no one is voicing.) Talk with your spouse about relevant, reachable goals. Record your real-world plan in this book. Commit to following through on these plans, and prepare to be held accountable.

5. *Follow up.* Don't let the life application drift away without action. Be accountable to the other couples in your group, and refer to previous "Live" sections often. Take time at the beginning of each new study to review. See how you're doing.

6. *Repeat* as necessary.

small-group study tips

After going through each week's study with your spouse, it's time to sit down with the other couples in your group and go deeper. Here are a few thoughts on how to make the most of your small-group discussion time.

Set ground rules. You don't need many. Here are two:

First, you'll want couples in your group to commit to the entire eight-week study. A binding legal document with notarized signatures and commitments written in blood probably isn't necessary. Just remember this: Significant personal growth happens when group members spend enough time together to really get to know each other. Hit-and-miss attendance rarely allows this to occur.

Second, agree together that everyone's story is important. Time is a valuable commodity, so if you have an hour to spend together, do your best to give each person ample time to express concerns, pass along insights, and generally feel like a participating member of the group. Small-group discussions are not monologues. However, a one-person-dominated discussion isn't always a bad thing. Not only is your role in a small group to explore and expand your own understanding, it's also to support one another. If someone truly needs more of the floor, give it to her. There will be times when the needs of the one outweigh the needs of the many. Use good judgment and allow a person extra time when needed. Your time may be next week.

Meet regularly. Choose a time and place, and stick to it. No one likes to arrange for a sitter, only to arrive at the study and learn that the meeting was canceled because someone's out of town. Consistency removes stress that could otherwise frustrate discussion and personal growth. It's only eight weeks. You can do this.

Talk openly. If you enter this study with shields up, you're probably not alone. And you're not a "bad person" for hesitating to unpack your life in front of friends or strangers. Maybe you're skeptical about the value of revealing the deepest parts of who you are to others. Maybe you're just not ready to say that much about that aspect of your marriage. Really, you don't have to go to a place where you're uncomfortable. If you want to sit and listen, offer a few thoughts, or merely hint at dilemmas in your marriage, go ahead. But don't neglect what brings you to this group of couples—that longing for a better, more satisfying, less tension-filled marriage. Dip your feet in the water of brutally honest conversation and you may choose to dive in. There is healing here.

Stay on task. Refrain from sharing information that falls into the "too much information" category. Don't spill unnecessary stuff, such as your wife's penchant for midnight belly dancing or your husband's obsession with Sandra Bullock.

If structure isn't your group's strength, try a few minutes of general comments about the study, and then take each "Live" question one at a time and give everyone in the group a chance to respond. That should quickly get you into the meat of matters.

Hold each other accountable. That "Live" section isn't just busywork. If you're ready for positive change in your marriage, take this section seriously. Not only should you be thorough as you summarize your discoveries, practical as you compose your goals, and realistic as you determine the plan for accountability, you must also hold the other couples in the group accountable for doing these things. Be lovingly, brutally honest as you examine each other's "Live" section. Don't hold back—this is where the rubber meets the road. A lack of openness here may send other couples in your group skidding off that road.

strategic or spontaneous?

"Why deliberately plan our marriage? Isn't there room for a little spontaneity now and then?"

the beginning place

Man is a goal seeking animal. His life only has meaning if he is reaching out and striving for his goals.

—ARISTOTLE

Wasn't marriage, like life, unstimulating and unprofitable and somewhat empty when too well ordered and protected and guarded? Wasn't it finer, more splendid, more nourishing, when it was, like life itself, a mixture of the sordid and the magnificent; of mud and stars; of earth and flowers; of love and hate and laughter and tears and ugliness and beauty and hurt?

—EDNA FERBER

It strikes some as a cruel cosmic joke that these two voices, strategic and spontaneous, are reflected in the typical marriage—one spouse striving for goals just beyond his reach, the other relishing the splendid messiness of her reality. It is difficult to pin down whether it has always been this way, or if now even our marriages—as entertainment, sports, and churches have already done—are patterning themselves after business-management principles.

But, you may say, a marriage is not a business—it is a relationship, and a highly fluid one at that, even within the stasis of monogamy. Who doesn't appreciate—yea, need—some whimsy and spontaneity and romantic impertinence in their marriage? Especially during the current Age of Schedules, when child-rearing trends, instant communication, job insecurity, and overwork have all converged at your marriage. Your 401(k) manager tells you to plan for your retirement. E-mail spam tells you to take control of your sex life. Your boss reminds you to manage your time well. Your pastor presses you to take control of your spiritual growth, your family's spiritual growth, your finances—and your sex life. You cannot even take respite in your own kitchen, for the refrigerator door exhorts you to remember soccer practices, doctor appointments, school meetings, and insurance payments.

So where is the joy, the fun, the spontaneity? The issue becomes one of degree. At what point does a couple living a carefree marriage begin to sacrifice, jettison, discard, or ignore some things essential for a healthy marriage? For coexisting with the very real need for impulsiveness in a marriage, for leaving at least a few loose ends just to see what adventures they'll lead to, is the need for intentionality, deliberateness, decision making, planning, goal setting.

One reason for being blatantly intentional is that with so much drifting about in a marriage—jobs that come and go, children who become different people every few years, the fluctuating demands of friendships and extended family and church—with all this swashing around of stuff that resists being planned and scheduled and made predictable, it's all the more critical that you be intentional and strategic about those few things you *can* be intentional and strategic about. Such islands of certainty can become calm, quiet havens when everything else in your life gets stormy.

Too, if you're hardwired for goal setting and strategic planning, it all comes naturally. If you're *not* wired for it—if you are by nature spontaneous and Let's See Where This Day Will Take Us—then you'll have to work at being deliberate, at least in those domestic arenas where it is most important. All the more so if you're married to someone who *is* hardwired for intentional planning and goal setting—a spouse who could become frustrated by what she perceives as marital aimlessness.

Then there's the argument for deliberateness advanced by motivational speaker John Scherer, who was heard in a workshop to boldly aver, "Planning is priceless; the plan is useless." Which is to say, even if all those plans and goals the two of you agree on have to be constantly tweaked, overhauled beyond recognition, or simply dropped, just the process of planning was worth it. You talked with each other, you communicated your dreams and visions, and in so doing you strengthened your marriage. Even if the plans fell through.

So if you relish the management angle of your marriage, *why* do you relish it? If you dread it and avoid it, why? How does your spouse respond to your feelings about managing the details of your marriage? If your marriage is not characterized by strategic planning, what fuels it for the long haul? If you *do* make space for intentional goal setting, why? And what role does spontaneity have in your marriage? Use the space below to summarize your beginning place for this lesson. Describe why you don't spend time with your spouse in managing the direction of your marriage, or why you do—and the effects on your marriage of planning or not planning. We'll start here and then go deeper.

read   a little ancient light on the subject

Why plan, anyway? (from Proverbs)

> Foolish dreamers live in a world of illusion;
>> wise realists plant their feet on the ground. (14:18)

> Form your purpose by asking for counsel,
>> then carry it out using all the help you can get. (20:18)

> Careful planning puts you ahead in the long run;
>> hurry and scurry puts you further behind. (21:5)

> Strategic planning is the key to warfare;
>> to win, you need a lot of good counsel. (24:6)

> First plant your fields;
>> *then* build your barn. (24:27)

think

- Which of these adages connects most directly with you? Why?
- Do Bible verses like these make you feel affirmed or a little chagrined? Why?
- Is it a stretch or is it common sense to say that Proverbs 20:18 is a good, solid, biblical reason for even happily married people to get marriage counseling? Talk about this.
- Write your own proverb to add to this list, using images from your own life and contexts.

think (continued)

pray

read   and in the spirit of full disclosure . . .

The other side of being purposeful (from Proverbs)

Mortals make elaborate plans,
>but God has the last word. (16:1)

We plan the way we want to live,
>but only God makes us able to live it. (16:9)

Make your motions and cast your votes,
>but God has the final say. (16:33)

We humans keep brainstorming options and plans,
>but God's purpose prevails. (19:21)

think

- How do you reconcile the biblical teaching in *these* verses with the biblical teaching in Proverbs of the previous reading on page 18?
- How do these proverbs make you feel about planning, casting votes, and brainstorming about issues in your marriage?
- If God has the final say, how deeply should you—*can* you—be deliberate about planning the many aspects of your marriage?

think (continued)

pray

read   monarchs of your own kingdom

From *The Good Marriage: How and Why Love Lasts*, by Judith Wallerstein and Sandra Blakeslee[1]

By building togetherness and autonomy, I mean putting together a shared vision of how you want to spend your lives together— constructing the psychological identity of the marriage as an entity in itself. The adolescent and the young adult are fundamentally "me"-centered, for a person at this stage is chiefly engaged in establishing his or her identity separate from the family of origin. Building the new, shared identity of marriage requires a shift from the "I" of the emancipated adolescent and young adult to a solid and lasting "we." At the same time the sense of we-ness has to include room for the autonomy of each partner. In couples who divorce, this we-ness is often weak or absent altogether.

The sense of being part of a couple is what consolidates modern marriage. It is the strongest rampart against the relentless threat of our divorce culture. We-ness gives marriage its staying power in the face of life's inevitable frustrations and temptations to run away or stray. It also gives the partners a sense that they constitute a sovereign country in which they make all the rules. People cannot usually choose what time to go to work or school, but they can determine what goes on inside their marriage. Within the civilization they create, they can exert true control.

think

- On a scale of 1 (extreme "I-ness") to 10 (extreme "we-ness"), point out where you feel your spouse is in this season.
- Has your spouse significantly shifted along this spectrum since your marriage began? If so, which way?
- Do you feel as empowered in the sovereign country of your own marriage as these writers say you should? Why or why not?
- How far along are the two of you in creating your private civilization? What are the most obvious characteristics of this

civilization? Did you intentionally and deliberately plan to create these characteristics, or did one or both of you simply bring them into the marriage, or did these characteristics just show up one day?

pray

read   sweat equity in one's marriage

From *Loving Your Wife: Strengthening Your Marriage in a Fallen World*, by
Jack and Cynthia Heald[2]

To be skilled in any trade involves a lifelong commitment to
excellence, not just a short apprenticeship. I want to be a work-
man approved by God in my knowledge of and skill in applying
His principles to my life and marriage. All of this requires time,
discipline, and perseverance. In 1964 I asked God to show me
how His Word was valuable for my life twenty-four hours a day,
seven days a week. What little I know now has been more than
adequate. I want to know more of Him, and I want Him to be my
source of wisdom to build, establish, and fill my life, marriage,
and home. I am excited at the prospect that men today can have
the vision for their lives that Ezra, the prophet, had: "For Ezra has
set his heart to study the law of the Lord, and to practice it, and
to teach His statutes and ordinances in Israel" (Ezra 7:10). I know
that I want my teaching to be first by the example of a commitment to God and to my marriage.

think

- What do the writers say is of first importance in planning their
  marriage?
- Compare that with what an objective observer would say is of
  apparent first importance in the planning of *your* marriage.
- "Time, discipline, and perseverance"—in the planning of your
  marriage, which of these three are you the strongest in? The
  weakest? How about your spouse?
- To those people beyond your immediate family, among whom
  you spend most of your time—probably coworkers, relatives,
  or friends—how significant is your marriage in their estima-
  tion of your faith? Why?

think (continued)

pray

read   stalker

From *Pilgrim at Tinker Creek*, by Annie Dillard[3]

The old, classic rule for stalking is, "Stop often 'n' set frequent." The rule cannot be improved upon, but muskrats will permit a little more. If a muskrat's eyes are out of sight, I can practically do a buck-and-wing on his tail, and he'll never notice. A few days ago I approached a muskrat feeding on a bank by the troll bridge simply by taking as many gliding steps towards him as possible while his head was turned. I spread my weight as evenly as I could, so that he wouldn't feel my coming through the ground, and so that no matter when I became visible to him, I could pause motionless until he turned away again without having to balance too awkwardly on one leg.

Stalking is a pure form of skill, like pitching or playing chess. Rarely is luck involved. I do it right or I do it wrong; the muskrat will tell me, and that right early. Even more than baseball, stalking is a game played in the actual present. At every second, the muskrat comes, or stays, or goes, depending on my skill.

think

- Stalking is hardly spontaneous; to the contrary, it is a picture of tenacious deliberateness. What is worth stalking in a marriage?
- "Rarely is luck involved. I do it right or I do it wrong; my spouse will tell me, and that right early." What in your marriage can you say that about?
- Critical in stalking, Dillard writes, is to "stop often 'n' set frequent." When it comes to your marriage, to what purpose would you want to stop and sit frequently?
- If you feel at least somewhat successful at marriage, how much of your success do you attribute to practical, practiced, learned skills—as opposed to, say, your nature, your personality, your natural tendencies? What skills, do you believe, would serve you well if you learned them?

think (continued)

pray

read   the irresolute husband

From *Babbitt*, by Sinclair Lewis[4]

With the assistance of Tanis's Bunch, the Doppelbraus, and other companions in forgetfulness, there was not an evening for two weeks when he did not return home late and shaky. With his other faculties blurred he yet had the motorist's gift of being able to drive when he could scarce walk; of slowing down at corners and allowing for approaching cars. He came wambling into the house. If Verona and Kenneth Escott were about, he got past them with a hasty greeting, horribly aware of their level young glances, and hid himself up-stairs. He found when he came into the warm house that he was hazier than he had believed. His head whirled. He dared not lie down. He tried to soak out the alcohol in a hot bath. For the moment his head was clearer but when he moved about the bathroom his calculations of distance were wrong, so that he dragged down the towels, and knocked over the soap-dish with a clatter which, he feared, would betray him to the children. . . . To hide his "condition" from his own children! To have danced and shouted with people whom he despised! To have said foolish things, sung idiotic songs, tried to kiss silly girls! . . . As it came relentlessly back to him he snarled, "I hate myself! God, how I hate myself!" But, he raged, "I'm through! No more! Had enough, plenty!"

He was even surer about it the morning after, when he was trying to be grave and paternal with his daughters at breakfast. At noontime he was less sure. He did not deny that he had been a fool; he saw it almost as clearly as at midnight; but anything, he struggled, was better than going back to a life of barren heartiness. At four he wanted a drink. He kept a whisky flask in his desk now, and after two minutes of battle had had his drink. Three drinks later he began to see the Bunch as tender and amusing friends, and by six he was with them . . . and the tale was to be told all over.

✳✳✳

Mrs. Babbitt returned in August.

On her previous absences he had missed her reassuring buzz and of her arrival he had made a fête. Now, though he dared not hurt her by letting a hint of it appear in his letters, he was sorry that she was coming before he had found himself, and he was embarrassed by the need of meeting her and looking joyful.

He loitered down to the station; he studied the summer-resort posters, lest he have to speak to acquaintances and expose his uneasiness. But he was well trained. When the train clanked in he was out on the cement platform, peering into the chair-cars, and as he saw her in the line of passengers he embraced her, and announced, "Well, well, well, well, by golly, you look fine, you look fine." Then he was aware of Tinka. Here was something, this child with her absurd little nose and lively eyes, that loved him, believed him great, and as he clasped her, lifted and held her till she squealed, he was for the moment come back to his old steady self.

Tinka sat beside him in the car, with one hand on the steering-wheel, pretending to help him drive, and he shouted back to his wife, "I'll bet the kid will be the best chuffer in the family! She holds the wheel like an old professional!"

All the while he was dreading the moment when he would be alone with his wife and she would patiently expect him to be ardent.

think

- What declarations have you ever made about your marriage, only to see your vows melt away after a day or two?
- Alcohol dissolves Babbitt's good intentions. What is it with you?
- If Mr. and Mrs. Babbitt came to you for marriage advice, what would you suggest?
- What details of marital management has Babbitt neglected? Have *you* neglected?

think (continued)

pray

LIVE

what i want to discuss

What have you discovered this week that you definitely want to discuss with your small group? Write that here. Then begin your small-group discussion with these thoughts.

so what?

Use the following space to summarize what you've discovered during this chapter about the need to be both strategic and spontaneous in your marriage. Review your Beginning Place if you need to remember where you began. How does God's truth impact the next step in your journey?

then what?

What is one practical thing you can do to apply what you've discovered? Describe how you will put this into practice. What steps will you take? Remember to think realistically; an admirable but unreachable goal is as good as no goal. Discuss your goal with your small group to further define it.

how?

Identify how you will be held accountable to the goal you described. Who will be on your support team? What are their responsibilities? How will you measure the success of your plan? Write the details here.

details, details

"What exactly needs management in our marriage—I mean,
besides making sure bills get paid?"

the beginning place

The only way not to think about money is to have a great deal
of it.

—EDITH WHARTON

If it's an enduring marriage you want, then it may be worth your while
to spend some time considering (without necessarily dwelling on) why
marriages fail. If the devil is in the details, then what details are so
neglected, overlooked, slighted, or ignored that one spouse wants out?

Money typically heads the list—not having enough, perceptions of
a spouse not doing enough to earn more, one's socioeconomic level
lower than what he was raised with (often with ensuing resentment
that lands on the spouse), conflicting ideas on how to solve financial
problems. Another top reason marriages break down is unmet needs,
especially the need for communication. Then there's a dramatic change

in priorities—a change not shared by both partners—and a lack of commitment to the marriage, whether expressed by outright infidelity or by any one of those dozens of little oversights and unkindnesses that are no less fatal to a marriage than an affair can be.

Okay, so if these are the typical stress points in a marriage, then perhaps here also is where some deliberate planning and management of details are needed. Take, for instance, Gwen and Pat's marriage of two decades. The two of them have very different perceptions of money. Pat has always tended to be worried about money, frugal to the point of anxiety. While most people only wince at the occasional parking ticket or overdraft fee, Pat gets a little panicky: "We might as well have just taken a twenty-dollar bill and lit it on fire!" And he almost needs to be kidnapped in order to take a rare weekend pleasure trip to the coast, because he's convinced they can't afford it.

Gwen, meanwhile, believes that money comes, money goes, the bills are always there to be paid, they always somehow get paid, life is short, and she and Pat need to get away every now and then. She's not rash with money, not a spendthrift. She knows how to skimp and thrift-shop as well as Pat, but to her the spending of money is a means to enhance important relationships every now and then. To Pat the spending of money is a slippery slope that ends in penury.

So what kind of deliberate planning and strategy setting must occur in this marriage before money escalates from a difference to a divorce? Plan ahead for twice-a-year weekend trips so Pat has a chance to put money aside for them instead of feeling that they're spending money better used for bills? Or perhaps make an appointment with a financial counselor so Pat and Gwen can both hear from an impartial source that, actually, they're not doing too bad financially, all things considered—and also a couple tips to improve their situation here and there.

Or take the stress point of communication. What details need specific attention by both partners in order to keep this from becoming a widening wedge between them? What about their communication with each other needs to be deliberated, managed, evaluated? Go to bed at the same time and debrief the day there? Rise at the same time in order

to breakfast together? Institute a Saturday-morning coffee time for planning the week? Hire a high schooler from the church youth group to
show up every Tuesday at six to babysit so you and your spouse can
count on at least *one* evening a week just to yourselves?

So what are the stress points in your marriage, and what details
in those areas need attention, planning, some intentionality? Is your
growing family beginning to require attention to details? What details in
each of your daily schedules need trimming, watering, nurturing? Use
the space below to summarize your beginning place for this lesson.
Describe those aspects of your marriage that need some intentional,
deliberate planning and why one of you (or both of you) tends to avoid
such planning. We'll start here and then go deeper.

read   easy for *her* to say

From amazon.com Spotlight Review "Neither Revolutionary nor Visionary," by reader Cade Foster[1]

I gave this book two stars because I think the author makes a couple of valuable points. Yes, parents (both mothers *and* fathers) need to make an investment in their children, rather than viewing marriage primarily as a way of bettering their own economic status. Children need to be viewed as something other than status symbols for parents, like luxury cars.

But the veiled insults to men—and women who don't follow her get-married-have-babies-have-career timetable—outweigh any positive contributions this book may have to make. Speaking from my own marriage . . . my wife and I are both concerned about having enough time with our children, as well as making ends meet. The author seems to forget that marrying and having children too young (and unlike her, I actually did) is not only a prescription for disaster, but virtually guarantees that the child will be raised in poverty. Having young parents and grandparents is not much consolation to a child if the parents are constantly worried about cash. I am a Christian, a conservative, and believe children are a blessing, but thirty-two is a lot better than twenty-two unless you've married a millionaire. Most of us don't have that opportunity. (Somehow, I also doubt that she wrote this entire book during her children's nursery school hours and nap-time.)

What bothers me the most about these books is that they attempt to present a handbook for the "correct" way to live. I have news for them: There isn't one. Some women are single by choice, just as some men are. Some younger marriages don't work out and some do. A marriage is a partnership, and how spouses allocate those responsibilities is their business. Danielle Crittenden got lucky—her lifestyle works for her. For heavens' sake, she should count her blessings and *not* wonder why the rest of us don't live the way she does.

think

- What details in the parenting life of this reviewer have required deliberate, intentional planning? What did he feel might have needed more planning than it received?
- Do you feel lucky in your lifestyle—married, single, kids, no kids, job, whatever—or do you feel under pressure of some sort (or of several sorts)? Talk about this.
- If you feel pressure—around parenting your children, say—would strategic planning with your spouse about parenting help relieve any of that pressure? Or do you feel that it's just life, or at least a life phase, and that you simply need to gut it out and endure?

pray

read   don't fret, focus!

Matthew 6:33-34

> "Steep your life in God-reality, God-initiative, God-provisions. Don't worry about missing out. You'll find all your everyday human concerns will be met.
>
> "Give your entire attention to what God is doing right now, and don't get worked up about what may or may not happen tomorrow. God will help you deal with whatever hard things come up when the time comes."

think

- What's your sense about these words of Jesus: that they underline the importance of deliberately planning your life, or that they minimize the need of such planning? Why?
- What, if any, details does Jesus seem to want us to focus on?
- During what past episode or season in your marriage do you wish you had known these verses? Talk about this.

think (continued)

pray

read   couples, choose your rules.

Ezekiel 43:10

> Son of man, tell the people of Israel all about the Temple. . . . Get
> them to go over the layout. . . . Show them the whole plan of the
> Temple, its ins and outs, the proportions, the regulations, and the
> laws. Draw a picture so they can see the design and meaning and
> live by its design and intent.

From *Becoming a Couple of Promise*, by Kevin Leman[2]

Most of us carry around some guidelines—mostly unspoken
—about how we ought to communicate with our spouses. We
have some definite ideas about what is appropriate and what is
good in a marital conversation. But let's get more specific about a
few standard rules that anyone can apply in order to foster good
communication.

Don't go to bed mad. You'll find this bit of common-sense advice
clearly stated in the Bible: "In your anger do not sin. Do not let
the sun go down while you are still angry" (Ephesians 4:26).

In other words, a mad bed is a bad bed. If there's something
bothering you, it's best to get it out on the table as soon as possible. Going to bed with bitterness and frustration only keeps
tensions running high in the marriage. And if held in over a long
period of time, when the problem does finally surface it's more
likely to gush out in a dam burst of accusation and personal
attack. That's just not necessary.

Keep your feelings warm. One day two ice fishermen were out
trying their luck. The young guy watched the senior citizen pull-
ing up fish after fish through the small hole in the ice. The young
man yelled over to the old-timer, "What's your secret?"

He mumbled something back.

"I said, 'What's your secret?'"

He mumbled again.

"What?"

The elderly man then spit out a small, brown, wiggly mass into his hand. "You gotta keep your worms warm!"

In the same fashion, I'm here to suggest: You've got to keep feelings warm in a marriage. Don't let them go stale. Even if you've got conflicts, work them out together passionately. It's always better to be fully engaged than to clam up and walk away from each other—either physically or emotionally.

Deal directly with anger. First, it's important to recognize that anger is a valid emotion. We can't just say to ourselves: *Don't feel that way.* When anger is there, it's there. The issue is how we handle it and what we do with it. Go back and reread Ephesians 4:26. The apostle Paul has no problem recognizing that anger will occur. In fact, you'll recall that Jesus got angry. He charged the temple and overturned the tables of the moneychangers in a fit of righteous rage (see John 2:12-25).

Remember, however, this was the same man who preached turning the other cheek. Just as Ecclesiastes 3 declares that there is a time for every purpose under the heavens, there is a time to turn the other cheek and also a time to pull the rug out from under the one who's attempting to avoid personal responsibility for wrong actions. Our anger can spur us to confront problems head-on, keeping responsibility where it belongs.

While validating anger and action, Ephesians 4:26 also warns us about the potential for sinning in the midst of such strong feelings. Putting a lid on our anger, letting it go stale, so to speak, instead of keeping it warm and dealing with it right at the proper time, can actually open us up to sin.

think

- Marital details that need intentional planning aren't just administrative details, so to speak (division of labor, household tasks, and such). Intangibles, such as your communication, also require deliberation and decision making. Leman advocates adopting rules and regs for communicating with each other. What are your first impressions of his list?

- If the two of you have found a workable way to communicate with each other, especially in chilly or hot conflict, did you slide into it, or did both of you intentionally devise such a plan? Talk about this.

- The Bible, according to Leman, requires promptly dealing with your anger (Ephesians 4), permits "righteous rage" (John 2), and acknowledges that there is a time for hating as well as for loving (Ecclesiastes 3). How do you incorporate such teaching into your marriage?

- What would your marriage look like if, to use the prophet Ezekiel's words, you planned with your spouse to "live by its design and intent"?

think (continued)

pray

read the fluctuations, alterations, and evolutions of a marriage

From *The Good Marriage: How and Why Love Lasts*, by Judith Wallerstein and Sandra Blakeslee[3]

Throughout the marriage husband and wife must make room—even if reluctantly—for change and for difference, for altering values, tastes, needs, and careers. Husband and wife continually confront the issue of how to reshape their shared identity so it continues to express what they want as a couple and what they need as individuals. Given the vast number of choices and trajectories, this challenge creates a never-ending tension in marriage.

Paradoxically, it is out of this push-pull of autonomy and togetherness that the couple acquires a sense of good emotional, moral, and cognitive fit. To reach the conclusion that the relationship is uniquely gratifying requires the meshing of both partners' conscious and unconscious wishes and needs and the acceptance of compromise as reasonably fair or at least temporarily necessary. To achieve this state, not only must each person feel free to make his or her wishes known but both must agree on what is fair. This agreement allows each one to accept disappointments without rage and take a fair portion in lieu of everything. It works only if the couple regards the well-being of the marriage as more important than the separate desires of either partner. The sense of what is fair is heavily influenced by the family of origin and the social milieu, but the final definition and modifications have to be worked out repeatedly in each marriage. In today's world each couple negotiates its own code of justice.

think

- Do you feel that your marriage is mutually gratifying, that it meshes the "conscious and unconscious wishes and needs" of both of you?
- What in your marriage are the details "for change, for altering values, tastes, needs, and careers"?
- Do you or your spouse feel the need to "reshape your shared identity so it continues to express what you want as a couple and what you need as individuals"? If so, what would be the first step (or stumble)?

pray

read   duped by love into marriage

From *Married: A Fine Predicament*, by Anne Roiphe[4]

You just never know, you never really know if the person you love is truly worthy of your affections or just a stand-in for some older pattern, some unfortunate primary mommy-daddy relationship in your life. Time reveals the answer. But we marry with risk, we marry the way a rock climber might put his foot on the next higher ledge, hopefully and with no alternatives in sight. When Titania falls in love with the ass due to some puckish mischief in *Midsummer's Night Dream*, she is duped by her emotions, unable to tell an ass from a fairy king. This mischief of course we usually do to ourselves as we fall in love and lose control of our judgment and marry in the heavy fog of one illusion or another. Love was personified in the classical world as the winged child Cupid wandering around with his sack of arrows. This image which has been transformed in modern times into the adorable cuteness of a valentine sent to a fifth-grade classmate nevertheless catches the ancient cruelty, the sharp point of the arrow, the randomness of its target, the indifferent playfulness of its intention. The idea of being shot with a sharp object is not how we might like to think of love. But the arrow which is usually restrained to the hunt or the battlefield is here used to convey the physical and mental assault that love brings in its wake. The lack of kindness, the lack of gentleness in this most turbulent of emotions and the vision of baby Cupid aiming his bow tells us exactly how childish an emotion love is, what a deep wound may follow.

think

- What in this passage particularly intrigues you? Why?
- If any of what Roiphe writes here is accurate, there are lots of details that need your deliberate attention if your marriage—begun "in the heavy fog of one illusion or another"—is to endure. What are some of those details?

- "We marry with risk," the author writes. What risks did your marriage begin with? How did intentional planning help reduce those risks—or, if you didn't engage in such planning, how could it have improved your marriage?

pray

read   little rituals for a lot of warmth

From *Becoming a Couple of Promise*, by Kevin Leman[5]

Keeping the Promise

1. Husbands, give extra hugs this week. Keep in mind that your goal is not sex.
2. Wives, try joining your husband in an activity he enjoys. Make sure it's one that you *don't* enjoy! Be his recreational helpmate.
3. As a couple, resolve not to split up at the next party or event that you attend together.
4. Wives, plan a romantic evening this week for your spouse. It doesn't have to be an expensive night out, but unearth the candles, turn on the soft music . . . (you get the idea).
5. Try this "He Said/She Said" discussion starter: Historically and culturally, society has portioned our roles to men and women in marriage. How do those roles match up with what you know of "her needs" and "his needs" in marriage?

think

- Which of these marriage-nurturing details appeal to you—which could you adopt or adapt?
- On the other hand, which of these simply don't fit your marriage? Why not?
- What details like these—rituals or deliberate practices—do you and your spouse have that cultivate emotional warmth between you?

think (continued)

pray

LIVE

what i want to discuss

What have you discovered this week that you definitely want to discuss with your small group? Write that here. Then begin your small-group discussion with these thoughts.

so what?

Use the following space to summarize what you've discovered during this chapter about discerning what details in your marriage need planning and deliberate, strategic attention. Review your Beginning Place if you need to remember where you began. How does God's truth impact the next step in your journey?

then what?

What is one practical thing you can do to apply what you've discovered? Describe how you will put this into practice. What steps will you take? Remember to think realistically; an admirable but unreachable goal is as good as no goal. Discuss your goal with your small group to further define it.

how?

Identify how you will be held accountable to the goal you described. Who will be on your support team? What are their responsibilities? How will you measure the success of your plan? Write the details here.

priorities

"What is important to us, anyway? *Really* important, and to *both* of us?"

the beginning place

Never let the other fellow set the agenda.

—James Baker III

The Law of Triviality . . . briefly stated, it means that the time spent on any item of the agenda will be in inverse proportion to the sum involved.

—C. Northcote Parkinson

Prepared by a meeting's leaders, an agenda informs participants what is important and implies what is unimportant. An agenda determines the meeting's priorities, at least until participants decide otherwise. And such course changes, away from the agenda, do not necessarily subvert a meeting. There is too much unpredictability during the meeting's voyage for the agenda to be much help out at sea: stormy disagreements, change of emotional weather, unexpected currents of resistance. An agenda has done its job admirably if it simply gets you out of the harbor and headed in the general direction of your destination, with perhaps a list of landmarks or waypoints to keep your eyes open for.

Baker and Parkinson describe starkly how *not* to set the agenda for the meeting called marriage—a long meeting, hopefully, provided you and your spouse settle upon an agenda in wiser ways than these. If you truly and consciously collaborate on it, the agenda for your marriage will reveal its priorities and indicate what the two of you believe is most important to you and your marriage.

For this is likely the first step in making strategic, intentional decisions about your marriage: determining what is important to you. So what *is* important to the two of you? Are there things that ought to be important to you but aren't? Why aren't they? And why do you feel they ought to be important?

Or turn that line of self-questioning on its head: Are there things that are important to you and your marriage but shouldn't be? What makes you feel that they shouldn't be as important as they are?

Have you been gradually influenced or suddenly pushed (by family, coworkers, church, neighbors) into valuing something? Upon reflection, do you actually, deeply value that something? If you demote it a level or two, what will be the cost to you, to your marriage?

Take TV, for example. Julia and David grew up in the '50s, when black-and-white television sets became the new family hearth. (The TV even replaced the dining table: TV trays allowed families to share their meals not with each other as much as with Jackie Gleason, Steve Allen, and Huntley and Brinkley.) During college they both grew out of the habit of watching TV, and when they got married they didn't even think about getting one. When babies began coming, their casual TV-lessness hardened into conviction: They definitely did not want their kids raised on the tube.

Until, that is, their third child entered high school. Julia and David decided that it was more important to have that teenage son at home, even watching television, than constantly leaving the house to watch TV at a friend's.

That change in priorities cost the household something, and not just money. Over the next decade, a TV became probably more prominent in their home than they wanted it to, especially since they could then hardly *not* buy a VCR, then a DVD player (which made obsolete the hundred or so videocassettes they had purchased over the years). But the invasion of electronic entertainment into their domesticity was worth it, they figure: With a TV in the house, that last son was a little more inclined to bring his friends over and hang out in his own house. (Now, with the kids grown and moved out, they're just saying no to TiVo and HDTV. But they live for Saturday-night Britcoms on PBS.)

So beyond TV (or no TV), what are your priorities for your marriage? Imagine a Venn diagram: What's important to you? What's important to your spouse? And what are the overlapping areas of shared priorities? What are some priorities that are *not* shared, that only one of you holds, but that may need exploration and eventual adoption by the other? Use the space below to summarize your beginning place for this lesson. We'll start here and then go deeper.

read   kiss it good-bye

Luke 14:28-33

"Is there anyone here who, planning to build a new house, doesn't first sit down and figure the cost so you'll know if you can complete it? If you only get the foundation laid and then run out of money, you're going to look pretty foolish. Everyone passing by will poke fun at you: 'He started something he couldn't finish.'

"Or can you imagine a king going into battle against another king without first deciding whether it is possible with his ten thousand troops to face the twenty thousand troops of the other? And if he decides he can't, won't he send an emissary and work out a truce?

"Simply put, if you're not willing to take what is dearest to you, whether plans or people, and kiss it good-bye, you can't be my disciple."

think

- How does setting priorities for your marriage cost you something?
- What exactly has it cost you in the past? What might it cost you in the future?
- Have you ever, in talking about priorities with your spouse, felt like you took a plan that was dearest to you and kissed it good-bye?

think (continued)

pray

read   what are your nonnegotiables?

From *The Questions to Ask Before You Jump into Bed*, by Laurie Seale[1]

A Deal-Breaker is an egregious violation against something you believe or something you value. Racism. Selfishness. Lackadaisical. Financially irresponsible. Slovenly. Just as Must Haves are unique to individuals, so are your Deal-Breakers. What is annoying to me may be amusing to you. What I consider inviolate and absolutely unforgivable you may consider tolerable. This is another reason why it is imperative to make a list according to you. Your Deal-Breaker List will be gospel according to you. This is not your best friend's list. And not your mom's list.

Every person has her own list of things that are absolutely, under no condition even remotely tolerable.

Most Frequently Cited Deal-Breakers:
Qualities We Absolutely Cannot Tolerate in a Partner
- Financially irresponsible
- Procrastinates
- Parsimonious
- Unable to achieve balance in life—TV junkie/golf or shopping addict
- Recklessness
- Unreliable
- Punctuality/tardiness
- Lack of communication
- Inflexible/rigid
- Lack of self-awareness
- Obsessively analytical
- Fear of risk
- Righteous
- Unhappy with immediate family
- Denies self-responsibility
- Workaholic

- Worrier
- Religious incompatibility
- Spiritually intolerant
- Spiritually indifferent

Money
- What does money mean to you?
- Are you a saver or a spender? In what areas?
- Do you overdraw your bank account? For what reasons?
- How would you get yourself out of a financial predicament?
- Do you balance your checkbook? How often? To the nearest hundred? Nearest ten? To the penny?
- Do you carry cash or credit cards?
- What's your credit limit? Emotionally? Financially? Is it maxed out? If yes, was it worth it?
- How do your spending habits reflect your values?
- What does the greatest percentage of your money go towards?
- How much money do you need to be happy? Weekly? Monthly? Annually? Lifetime?

think

- Although this list was created for people looking for a spouse, what about it is relevant for those who already have a spouse—and a spouse they plan to keep for a long, long time? What about it strikes you as irrelevant to people already married?
- If you had to arrange the first list in order of importance to you, what would be your top three? Your bottom three?
- Because money, its uses, and disagreements about it figure so largely in a marriage, the author gave that topic its own battery of questions. Answer two of the questions to your spouse's satisfaction.

think (continued)

pray

read   easy as one, two, three, four

Adapted from "Priorities: Family, Self, Work, Spouse," by Paul Mauchline[2]

Prioritize the following four items (listed in alphabetical order):

- Career (or work)
- Family (including any children)
- Self
- Spouse (or partner)

When you are faced with the challenges of your daily life, I believe that the answer to the question "What truly are your priorities for life?" will help you to make better decisions and, more importantly, more conscious choices for yourself and your loved ones.

I have asked this thought-provoking question to thousands of people over the years, and I have heard many varied answers to the question. In many cases an individual immediately becomes defensive, trying to change the question—especially when two members of a couple discover that their answers are totally different. The question brings out resentment, hurt, emotional baggage, and fear—things that many people have kept hidden from their partners and, primarily, from themselves.

I asked this question of myself for the first time when I was in my late thirties, after I had been through several relationships. I only wish someone had posed this question to me years earlier. It would have saved me a lot of emotional pain and anguish. Finally asking it of myself initiated a change in my own life priorities.

At this point in my life, my priorities are the following:

1. Self
2. Spouse
3. Family
4. Work

Why do I put myself first? Quite simply: I cannot truly love my spouse or partner—or anyone else, for that matter—unless I love myself first.

And why do I place my spouse or partner second, before family and children? Because the example of my love for spouse or partner is the most important gift I can bestow upon my children and family.

And why is family and children third in my priorities? Because of my love for them: they are far more important than my work, far more important than any amount of material reward I receive as a result of my work. Loving myself, then my spouse, and then my family makes my work all that much more enjoyable and rewarding.

think

- Have you ever sat down and prioritized those four areas of your life (career, family, self, spouse)? Talk about that process, including how long it lasted and any ongoing results.
- Does this writer's process of setting priorities strike you as unrealistically simplistic, or helpfully simple?
- Can you imagine—or have you experienced—a season when your priorities were very different from, if not opposite of, the writer's own priorities?

think (continued)

pray

read biblical bases for your marriage's priorities

From *Becoming a Couple of Promise*, by Kevin Leman[3]

A Christian marriage and family life can be a wonderful witness to the ways of God. This is the second building block of the marital foundation. Right in our family we can demonstrate what God had in mind for human relationships. But we must be clear about exactly what we're aiming to convey.

If you go to business seminars, you usually hear all about goals and targets and objectives. But do families have goals today? If not, maybe it's because we have so little time to develop a clear sense of direction. Sixty percent of married women work outside the home, a situation that creates instant stress for your family and robs it of valuable time. Seven- and eight-year-olds now show up regularly in shrinks' offices because they're already stressed out. So we need to learn to ask ourselves the kinds of questions that will help us sort out our priorities. These are the hard questions like: What are our family's goals? Do we really have time for *this* activity or *that* commitment? And if we're going to make time for the things that matter the most to us, what things are we going to boot out?

Tough questions! And maybe they're so hard because they center on the values you're choosing for your home. If you're going to make it in marriage today, you've got to have a marriage that's full of priorities, all based on your most prized values.

Do you proclaim Christlike values—and live by them? Every family is unique, but the Scriptures [following] describe some of the virtues that you and your spouse might want to make priorities in your home. Skim through these passages and talk about them together for a few moments. Then identity the values that come through.

SCRIPTURE	*VALUE*
Deuteronomy 31:6	
Ruth 1:16-17	
Psalm 15	
Psalm 133:1	
Jonah 3	
John 13:35	
2 Corinthians 2:9	
2 Corinthians 8:6-7	
2 Thessalonians 3:6-13	
Hebrews 11:1-2	
James 1:2-5	
2 Peter 1:5-9	

think

- Which one or two values that you gleaned from the Bible passages resonate most deeply with you? Why do you suppose they do?
- Which passages do you find the least relevant to your marriage?
- If you and your spouse have already consciously assigned priorities to your marriage, what is one? Is it reflected in this list?

think (continued)

pray

read needed: an early warning system for conflicting priorities

From "Rules of Engagement," by Sandra G. Boodman[4]

While many engaged couples sign up for counseling to reduce the risk of future problems, therapists also see unmarried couples who are already having serious difficulties.

[Social worker Rob] Scuka estimates that 10 to 20 percent of premarital couples he works with decide to break up. "One of our jobs is to reinforce for a couple that they are making the right decision by getting married—or that this is potentially a big mistake," he said.

Often one partner, usually the woman, is having doubts she wants to air or is seeking help extricating herself from a doomed union. The most common issue, said [the founder of PREP, a premarital counseling program], is "conflict that isn't going well—that's a big one," followed by significant and seemingly irreconcilable differences in background, values or whether to have children.

think

- How influential in your decision to marry were each of your personal priorities?
- If you had premarital counseling, how much of it was devoted to articulating and comparing your individual priorities and then crafting priorities for your marriage?
- Have any of the rough patches in your marriage been due primarily to a difference in priorities? If you can, talk about this.

think (continued)

pray

read   just shuffling along

Colossians 3:1-2

> So if you're serious about living this new resurrection life with
> Christ, *act* like it. Pursue the things over which Christ presides.
> Don't shuffle along, eyes to the ground, absorbed with the things
> right in front of you. Look up, and be alert to what is going on
> around Christ—that's where the action is. See things from *his*
> perspective.

think

- The immediate context of the apostle Paul's words here is, of
  course, the task of cultivating one's spiritual life. Any application, however, to the task of setting priorities in your marriage?
- What proportion of your days do you feel as though you're
  shuffling along, and what proportion as though you're looking
  up and alert?
- What—or whose—perspectives besides your own would benefit you in organizing your priorities? How would those other
  perspectives help?

think (continued)

pray

LIVE

what i want to discuss

What have you discovered this week that you definitely want to discuss with your small group? Write that here. Then begin your small-group discussion with these thoughts.

so what?

Use the following space to summarize what you've discovered during this chapter about exploring and articulating what's really important to both of you in your marriage. Review your Beginning Place if you need to remember where you began. How does God's truth impact the next step in your journey?

then what?

What is one practical thing you can do to apply what you've discovered? Describe how you will put this into practice. What steps will you take? Remember to think realistically; an admirable but unreachable goal is as good as no goal. Discuss your goal with your small group to further define it.

how?

Identify how you will be held accountable to the goal you described. Who will be on your support team? What are their responsibilities? How will you measure the success of your plan? Write the details here.

clashing models

"I grew up with parents who talked about everything. My husband's parents didn't talk, period. So how do the two of us plan anything?"

the beginning place

It's just one of many paradoxes you notice as you mature: As you and your spouse grow up and grow into your marriage, you change and become different people. And you don't change at all.

In between those two truths is a broad gray area—a zone into which you brought expectations early in your marriage, models you observed and absorbed in your family of origin. Only problem is, the way *you're* accustomed to managing a marriage is probably way different from that of your *spouse*.

Cases in point:

Iris was raised by parents who avoided hierarchical authority, instead steering their family toward community, consensus, and mutuality. Iris's mother and father did not train her to obey parental commands but rather attempted to attract Iris to collaborate and participate in the community of a functioning family. So to this day, a quarter century into Iris's own marriage, she still says to Lewis in the kitchen, "Do you want to chop some scallions for the salad?" Lewis used to reply, honestly,

"No thanks—I can live without them." Now, however, her husband knows that what Iris *means* is, "I'd like scallions in the salad—would you please chop some?" but she expresses that desire in a nonauthoritarian manner, unconsciously assuming that Lewis will readily enlist in Iris's oniony plan with an invitation rather than with a direct request. "Just tell me what you want, and I'll do it," Lewis protested early in their marriage.

A model can be brought home from the workplace as well as from a family of origin. Cocooned all day in a glass and steel office tower, Seth used to unconsciously bring home the same manner of planning that worked so well with colleagues in his department. The only problem was that the crisp delegation and action-oriented decision making that moved projects along on schedule at work only alienated Trina and the kids at home. It took him years to realize that he needed to somehow depressurize before he walked in the door at night and that how he ought to manage his family—in partnership with Trina, with fewer directives, and with more conversation than he was used to preceding a decision—was very different from how he managed a deadline-driven office team.

Different models of behavior can be as distinct as different cultures. Nancy was indignant and hurt when she discovered that some in-laws had seemingly excluded her from a casual family gathering. "It may have been an oversight," her husband said as gently as he could, "but can't they invite and not invite whomever they want?"

"Not in *my* world," declared Nancy. In her world—that is, in the world of her childhood—if there was a family event, everyone was invited and just about everyone came, regardless of occasional tiffs between relatives, regardless of who did or didn't get along. Family was family, and it was a tacit credo in Nancy's extended family of origin that you *never* excluded anybody.

So what models tend to clash in your marriage? What's the effect of that clash on intentional, strategic planning of your marriage? What different kinds of cultures do you and your spouse represent? When did the two of you first run up against the reality of your vastly different models of conducting a marriage? Use the space following to summarize your beginning place for this lesson. Describe some current plans and decisions that may be suffering because you and your spouse are still approaching marital strategies from way different habits of thinking and behaving. We'll start here and then go deeper.

read   touchy, touchy

From *Secret Longings of the Heart: Overcoming Deep Disappointment and Unfulfilled Expectations*, by Carol Kent[1]

> Some of us *feel* deeply, but we have great difficulty *telling* someone else our heartfelt emotions. If we don't ever voice our needs, hurts, joys, and dreams to others, we limit the potential closeness. Family background has a lot to do with this. People who grew up in a family that talked, touched, and laughed together find communicating at an intimate level much easier than people who were raised by "non-touchers" who didn't voice their affection and opinions.

think

- Did the household in which you were raised do a lot of touching (frequent hugs, kisses, snuggling), or did physical connection seem limited to handshakes and goodnight pecks? What family memories of this stand out the most?
- How about your spouse's family—touchers or non-touchers?
- In your experience, how, if at all, are touching and communicating related in a household? Does more of one necessarily mean more of the other?

think (continued)

pray

read did i marry a person or an illusion?

From *Middlemarch*, by George Eliot[2]

"Close the book now, my dear. We will resume our work to-morrow. I have deferred it too long, and would gladly see it complete. But you observe that the principle on which my selection is made, is to give adequate, and not disproportionate illustration to each of the theses enumerated in my introduction, as at present sketched. You have perceived that distinctly, Dorothea?"

"Yes," said Dorothea, rather tremulously. She felt sick at heart.

"And now I think that I can take some repose," said Mr. Casaubon. He lay down again and begged her to put out the lights. When she had lain down too, and there was a darkness only broken by a dull glow on the hearth, he said—

"Before I sleep, I have a request to make, Dorothea."

"What is it?" said Dorothea, with a dread in her mind.

"It is that you will let me know, deliberately, whether, in case of my death, you will carry out my wishes: whether you will avoid doing what I should deprecate, and apply yourself to do what I should desire."

Dorothea was not taken by surprise: many incidents had been leading her to the conjecture of some intention on her husband's part which might make a new yoke for her. She did not answer immediately.

"You refuse?" said Mr. Casaubon, with more edge in his tone.

"No, I do not yet refuse," said Dorothea, in a clear voice, the need of freedom asserting itself within her; "but it is too solemn—I think it is not right—to make a promise when I am ignorant what it will bind me to. Whatever affection prompted I would do without promising."

"But you would use your own judgment: I ask you to obey mine; you refuse."

"No, dear, no!" said Dorothea, beseechingly, crushed by opposing fears. "But may I wait and reflect a little while? I desire with my whole soul to do what will comfort you; but I cannot give any pledge suddenly—still less a pledge to do I know not what."

"You cannot then confide in the nature of my wishes?"

"Grant me till to-morrow," said Dorothea beseechingly.

"Till to-morrow then," said Mr. Casaubon.

From "Explorations in Marital and Family Therapy," by James L. Framo[3]

People do not marry people, not real ones anyway; they marry what they think the person is; they marry illusions and images. The exciting adventure of marriage is finding out who the partner really is.

think

- This fictitious *Middlemarch* couple obviously brought very different natures into their marriage, especially—as seen in this exchange—when it comes to decision making. What marriages are you aware of whose plans and decisions are so starkly unshared? What do you know of those couples' families of origin?
- What illusion do you suppose Casaubon married when he married Dorothea? How does this illusion differ from the actual Dorothea?
- Name one illusion *you* married when you married your spouse, or a former spouse.

think (continued)

pray

read   good cop, bad cop

From *Toward Commitment: A Dialogue about Marriage*, by Diane Rehm and John B. Rehm[4]

So here we were, two people who had come from extraordinarily different backgrounds, with totally different parenting styles as our models, and acting out what we knew because of our own parents' behavior toward us as individual children. John felt he was absolutely correct in defending his children's rights to make their own decisions, even if defending them meant opposing me. That was what his family of origin allowed—even expected—him to do. I, on the other hand, believed children should adhere to my directions without question. I was the person in charge. John was barely there. How dare he come home and overturn rules I had laid down? How dare he assume the role of "good guy" as soon as he walked in the door? How dare he disagree with me, in calling into question the only style of parenting I knew? And how dare he, after all, not act as my father did, by agreeing with every action my mother took? It felt like total betrayal, and led us both, out of our mutual frustration, to engage in ugly screaming scenes.

think

- What parenting style were *you* raised with? How about your spouse?
- Describe some recent family-management decision making regarding your children in the course of which your and your spouse's own upbringings became very obvious.
- If you have children, who tends to be the parenting "good guy"? The parenting "tough guy"? When you're planning and setting parenting goals for your kids, how do you get through (or over, or around) your different approaches to parenting?

- Recall the first time—or a recent time—you recognized that your anger, indignation, or resentment sprang from your expecting your spouse to respond in a specific situation as your parent had. What effect on family management and decision making has this phenomenon had?

pray

read   and we'll set the corn god here, just in case

Genesis 31:17-26,30-39,42

Jacob did it. He put his children and his wives on camels and gathered all his livestock and everything he had gotten, everything acquired in Paddan Aram, to go back home to his father Isaac in the land of Canaan.

Laban was off shearing sheep. Rachel stole her father's household gods. And Jacob had concealed his plans so well that Laban the Aramean had no idea what was going on—he was totally in the dark. Jacob got away with everything he had and was soon across the Euphrates headed for the hill country of Gilead.

Three days later, Laban got the news: "Jacob's run off." Laban rounded up his relatives and chased after him. Seven days later they caught up with him in the hill country of Gilead. That night God came to Laban the Aramean in a dream and said, "Be careful what you do to Jacob, whether good or bad."

When Laban reached him, Jacob's tents were pitched in the Gilead mountains; Laban pitched his tents there, too.

"What do you mean," said Laban, "by keeping me in the dark and sneaking off, hauling my daughters off like prisoners of war? . . . I understand. You left because you were homesick. But why did you steal my household gods?"

Jacob answered Laban, "I was afraid. I thought you would take your daughters away from me by brute force. But as far as your gods are concerned, if you find that anybody here has them, that person dies. With all of us watching, look around. If you find anything here that belongs to you, take it." Jacob didn't know that Rachel had stolen the gods.

Laban went through Jacob's tent, Leah's tent, and the tents of the two maids but didn't find them. He went from Leah's tent to Rachel's. But Rachel had taken the household gods, put them inside a camel cushion, and was sitting on them. When Laban had gone through the tent, searching high and low without finding a thing, Rachel said to her father, "Don't think I'm being disrespect-ful, my master, that I can't stand before you, but I'm having my period." So even though he turned the place upside down in his search, he didn't find the household gods.

Now it was Jacob's turn to get angry. He lit into Laban: "So what's my crime, what wrong have I done you that you badger me like this? You've ransacked the place. Have you turned up a single thing that's yours? Let's see it—display the evidence. Our two families can be the jury and decide between us.

"In the twenty years I've worked for you, ewes and she-goats never miscarried. I never feasted on the rams from your flock. I never brought you a torn carcass killed by wild animals but that I paid for it out of my own pocket—actually, you made me pay whether it was my fault or not. . . . If the God of my father, the God of Abraham and the Fear of Isaac, had not stuck with me, you would have sent me off penniless. But God saw the fix I was in and how hard I had worked and last night rendered his verdict."

think

- What evidence is there in this passage for the different reli-gious upbringings of Rachel and Jacob?
- How do you explain Rachel's attachment to paganism even while married to the son of a monotheistic patriarch?
- How have you and your spouse grown beyond your separate religious upbringings? How are you still affected by them?
- Recall a time when your and your spouse's different spiritual backgrounds hobbled your decision-making process about churches or other faith issues.

think (continued)

pray

read a marital phoenix from parents' ashes

From "Marrying Out of History," by Nell Casey[5]

We each inherit our own legacy of marriage, defining ourselves with or against our own parents' marriage. In this sense, children are given the chance to do the finishing work of an earlier generation, studying their parents' past and then making their way into the future. This doesn't always guarantee brighter outcomes. My own parents, for example, were determined not to imitate their parents. My mother wanted a deeper intimacy than she saw in her mother and father's marriage. She didn't really feel that they *knew* each other. Although they were a wonderful match physically, sharp and elegant, they didn't seem to take each other seriously as partners. . . . In the end, I think my parents may also have been a little too in love with their own eccentric story. Like some kind of emotional Minotaur, they were one-half self-mythologizing, one-half earnestly aching to pull their marriage back to a safe place. Finally unable to contain their bursting and opposing emotions, my parents' marriage blew apart.

And so I begin the next chapter, armed with their defeat but also with a strong sense of idealism. I do not believe the happiness I have found with Jesse is simply love as redemption, or retribution for an unhappy childhood, but I do believe my sturdy sense of commitment sprang, in part, from the wreck of my parents' marriage. I still carry the past with me, worrying in irrational ways that seem to date back to my young suspicions that something was wrong in our house, that something was about to go terribly wrong. There is no sense in trying to banish those emotions, rooted as strongly as they are in my history, but here also is a new chance, and I am going to take it.

"You learned from us," my mother once offered. "You shaped yourself against the grain of our unhappiness." I tend to think of it more as luck, as if I whirled around the dance floor a little recklessly and somehow ended up in the arms of the right man at the end of the night. But, truthfully, I think my happiness is

made up of some unknowable combination—as unknowable as
love itself—of work and circumstance. It has to do with my own
strong desire to level a shaky sense of family and the joyous luck
of meeting someone who so deeply suits me. Perhaps my own
modern childhood crisis has sent me backward, back beyond the
cynicism of recent times, seeking marriage in an old-fashioned
sense.

think

- Have you tended to model your marriage after your parents'
  marriage, or (in the writer's phrase) shape yours against the
  grain of theirs? Talk about this.
- How about your parents—do you have any way of knowing
  if they modeled their marriage after that of *their* parents, or if
  they reacted against it?
- How is your own imitating or reacting against your parents'
  marriage affecting you and your spouse's planning and decision making for the near and distant future?
- In what ways are you armed with your parents' defeat as well
  as a strong sense of idealism for your own marriage?

think (continued)

pray

read   and when you get on each other's
nerves . . .

1 Thessalonians 5:14-15

> Gently encourage the stragglers, and reach out for the exhausted,
> pulling them to their feet. Be patient with each person, attentive
> to individual needs. And be careful that when you get on each
> other's nerves you don't snap at each other. Look for the best in
> each other, and always do your best to bring it out.

think

- If you're the spouse who grew up in a communicative, coop-
  erative family, what insight or advice is there for you in this
  Bible passage?
- If you're the spouse who grew up in an uncommunicative
  family characterized by unilateral decisions handed down by
  one parent, what insight or advice here is there for *you?*

think (continued)

pray

LIVE

what i want to discuss

What have you discovered this week that you definitely want to discuss with your small group? Write that here. Then begin your small-group discussion with these thoughts.

so what?

Use the following space to summarize what you've discovered during this chapter about the very different planning and goal-setting models you and your spouse may have brought into your marriage. Review your Beginning Place if you need to remember where you began. How does God's truth impact the next step in your journey?

then what?

What is one practical thing you can do to apply what you've discovered? Describe how you will put this into practice. What steps will you take? Remember to think realistically; an admirable but unreachable goal is as good as no goal. Discuss your goal with your small group to further define it.

how?

Identify how you will be held accountable to the goal you described. Who will be on your support team? What are their responsibilities? How will you measure the success of your plan? Write the details here.

pre-acting

"We're tired of merely reacting to changes in our marriage. How can we 'pre-act' now and then—anticipate at least the predictable events down the road?"

the beginning place

Four steps to achievement: Plan purposefully. Prepare prayerfully. Proceed positively. Pursue persistently.

—WILLIAM ARTHUR WARD

Eighty percent of success is showing up.

—WOODY ALLEN

Your neighbors update you regularly on the unfolding disaster that is their lives: their motor home breaks down again, this time a thousand miles from home. They tore out a saturated living room carpet for the second time in five years, thanks to a leaky seam in the house that for some reason keeps defying patching. Their elderly dog is likely addicted to pain pills that nonetheless keep it oblivious to canine arthritis. You find their latest report hard to believe: A tenant offed himself in one of their investment properties, leaving a bloody mess they have to clean up next weekend. Then you saw a brief mention of the suicide in the back of your newspaper's metro section.

Behind closed doors, you and your spouse shake your heads in wonder. Can any one couple fall into bad luck so regularly and frequently as your neighbors?

Or *is* it bad luck? Maybe they subtly sabotage themselves, or leave themselves vulnerable, you speculate. Or perhaps they simply don't think ahead and merely react to the inevitable emergencies that erupt—out of the blue, it seems to them. You wonder if at least some of the emergencies don't flow directly from their lack of foresight, of planning, of taking precautions, of making decisions prior to the emergencies.

Woody Allen may have been thinking of career success, but his quip applies no less to marriage. What if most of being proactive and anticipating the vicissitudes of married life is just acting? Just not putting off decisions, no matter what you actually decide. Just showing up at the table with your spouse and making deliberate plans, however arbitrary you think the exercise is, however unnatural you feel in the process, however against the grain of your temperament it is to be intentional about planning your life together.

Regularly maintaining your family vehicles between road trips, making the hard decision to put down the dog, doing a more thorough job screening prospective tenants—such steps can keep your physical household humming more smoothly. Yet what about regular emotional maintenance of your marriage? What about anticipating and making intentional decisions about what the two of you see for your marriage just around the corner: kids leaving home (whether to kindergarten or to college); one or both of you perceptibly changing in your tastes, needs, or values; the yearning of one or both of you for another child, another car, another job?

Marriage and life have plenty of genuine surprises that few can predict. So it makes sense, concerning events and phases that are likely to occur in the course of a marriage, that couples would want to anticipate these surprises as much as possible, take some deliberate action ahead of time, and make some decisions that will at least prepare your marriage for the strain so it doesn't break down in the middle of everything.

So in your own marital experience, what kinds of predictable events or phases have you not anticipated and planned for as well as you wish you had? What have been the consequences? What still lies in the future of your marriage that you just might be able to plan for a little (or a lot)? Use the space below to summarize your beginning place for this lesson. We'll start here and then go deeper.

read how open are you to the influence of your spouse?

From *Ten Lessons to Transform Your Marriage*, by John M. Gottman, Julie Schwartz Gottman, and Joan DeClaire[1]

Another problem we perceived in Beth and Craig's marriage was Craig's unwillingness to accept influence from Beth. Our research shows that this problem—which is most common among husbands—can be harmful to a relationship. That's because it leads wives to become frustrated and angry, increasing the chances that they'll become highly critical and contemptuous—behaviors proven to be quite destructive in a marriage.

To find out if accepting influence is a challenge in your marriage, answer the following questions:

PARTNER A T/F		PARTNER B T/F
	1. I am really interested in my partner's opinions on our basic conflicts.	
	2. I usually learn a lot from my partner, even when we disagree.	
	3. I want my partner to feel that what he or she says really matters to me.	
	4. I generally want my partner to feel influential in this marriage.	
	5. I can listen to my partner.	
	6. My partner has a lot of basic common sense.	
	7. I try to communicate respect, even during our disagreements.	

PARTNER A T/F		PARTNER B T/F
	8. If I keep trying to convince my partner, I will eventually succeed.	
	9. I don't reject my partner's opinions out of hand.	
	10. My partner is not rational enough to take seriously when we discuss our conflicts.	
	11. I believe in lots of give and take in our discussions.	
	12. I am very persuasive, and usually can win arguments with my partner.	
	13. I feel I have an important say when we make decisions.	
	14. My partner usually has good ideas.	
	15. My partner is basically a great help as a problem solver.	
	16. I try to listen respectfully, even when I disagree.	
	17. My ideas for solutions are usually much better than my partner's ideas.	
	18. I can usually find something to agree with in my partner's position.	
	19. My partner is usually too emotional.	
	20. I am the one who needs to make the major decisions in this relationship.	

SCORING: *Give yourself one point for each "true" answer, except for items 8, 10, 12, 17, 19, 20. Then subtract one point for each "true" answer to items 8, 10, 12, 17, 19, 20. If you scored 6 or above, accepting influence is an area of strength in your marriage. If you scored below 6, you and your partner need to make improvements in your willingness to accept influence from each other.*

think

- What is your score? What is your spouse's score? What might the comparison of scores tell you about your marriage?
- A key to being proactive in your marriage, instead of merely reactive, may be knowing how susceptible you are to the influence of your spouse. Is your first response generally to accept such influence, or resist it? Would your spouse say differently?
- Does it seem to you mere stereotype or objective observation that wives generally are the ones who want change in their marriages and that husbands generally resist it? Does your marriage reflect this pattern?

think (continued)

pray

read   act, already! (gently, though.)

From *The Way of Life*, by Lao Tzu[2]

Rule a large country.

As small fish are cooked.

Can you govern your animal soul, hold to the One and never depart from it?

Can you throttle your breath, down to the softness of breath in a child?

Can you purify your mystic vision and wash it until it is spotless?

Can you love all your people, rule over the land without being known?

Can you be like a female, and passively open and shut heaven's gates?

Can you keep clear in your mind the four quarters of earth and not interfere?

Quicken them, feed them;

Quicken but do not possess them.

Act and be independent;

Be the chief but never the lord:

This describes the mystic virtue.

Luke 9:60-62

> Jesus refused. "First things first. Your business is life, not death. And life is urgent: Announce God's kingdom!"
>
> Then another said, "I'm ready to follow you, Master, but first excuse me while I get things straightened out at home."
>
> Jesus said, "No procrastination. No backward looks. You can't put God's kingdom off till tomorrow. Seize the day."

think

- One could say that there is no anticipation of and planning for life's twists and turns without being, in the words of Lao Tzu, "the chief but never the lord"—that is, learning how to exert influence without being overbearing. What might this suggest for your marriage?
- According to the gospel of Luke, what did Jesus say that echoed Lao Tzu's "mystic virtue" of six centuries earlier?
- About what aspects of your marriage have you not been putting first things first? How might you have failed in this or that respect at ruling the country of your marriage? About what would Jesus say, if he were sitting at the same table as you and your spouse, "Seize the day"?

think (continued)

pray

read   who are we again?

From *The Good Marriage: How and Why Love Lasts*, by Judith Wallerstein and Sandra Blakeslee[3]

[When children start moving out,] couples who have defined themselves largely as parents need to rethink who they are as individuals and what their togetherness consists of. Autonomy has a new meaning, especially for women. Those who have regarded taking care of children as their major job face an exciting and frightening set of questions: who shall I be now, and what shall I do with the rest of my life? Women who have not been at home full-time face major changes as well. Should they now make a greater investment in their career or spend more time in other activities?

All couples must confront once again the questions they faced as newlyweds: how much emotional investment do we make in us as a couple? How much time will we spend in activities with other people or in individual pursuits? The issues are all on the table again. These decisions will determine the nature of the relationship over the next decades. This transition is especially important because of our lengthening life span. The average life expectancy for a woman is now seventy-nine, and for a man, seventy-two. Many people live healthy, contented lives well into their eighties. And the quality of the marriage has a significant effect on physical and mental health during later years.

think

- Here is at least one big shift in your marriage that is plainly predictable: If you have children, how many years until the youngest turns 18? How do you picture your marriage with no kids in the house?
- What issues that you thought were settled earlier in your marriage do you find on the table again?

- What sorts of planning or decisions can the two of you make now that will smooth your marriage's empty-nest transition?

pray

read   dating, again

From *Loving Your Husband: Building an Intimate Marriage in a Fallen World*, by Cynthia Heald[4]

It is so easy to settle into roles, routines, and ruts in marriage. So often Jack and I are both tired in the evening and have little to give to one another because we have been giving to others (children included). Just as we schedule specific times to be with other friends, it is also necessary to plan time to be with our husbands.

For years I didn't think I should take the initiative to arrange any special times for us to be together. Finally, one day it dawned on me that I was the creative one in our relationship and it was all right for me to make suggestions and plans for our time together. (It was also a relief to Jack!) Our times together have included crackers and cheese after the children were in bed to relaxing weekends away.

It is in these special times that we can express our love and deepen its growth. A friend delights in planning and doing thoughtful things for loved ones. What kind of friend are you to your husband?

think

- It's not only the big picture of your marriage that needs planning and intentional management—sometimes it's the little things too. What little things about your relationship could use some deliberate forethought?
- What are your feelings about calendaring regular time with your spouse: too office-like for your tastes, or too important *not* to treat like a business appointment?
- Is one of you "the creative one" in your marriage? If so, do you both recognize it? What duties, permission, or relief might come with that role in your partnership?

think (continued)

pray

read   when the tiger claws at your door

From the *Utne* article "My Cheatin' Heart: When Love Comes Knocking, Do You Answer the Door?" by Daphne Gottlieb[5]

Out there in self-help books, on daytime television shows, I see people told that they're wrong to lust outside their relationships. That they must heal what's wrong at home and then they won't feel desire "inappropriately." I've got news. There's nothing wrong. Desire is not an illness. We who are its witnesses are not infected. We're not at fault. Not all of us are running away from our relationships at home, or just looking for some side action. The plain fact about desire is that sometimes it's love.

If it were anything else, maybe it would be easier. But things are not as simple as we were always promised. Let's say you're a normal, upstanding, ethical man (or woman) who has decided to share your life with someone beloved to you. This goes well for a number of years. You have a lot of sex and love each other very much and have a seriously deep, strong bond. Behind door number two, the tiger: a true love. Another one. (Let's assume for the moment that the culture and Hollywood are wrong—we have more than one true love after all.)

The [worst] thing you can do is lie to someone you love, yet there are certain times you can choose either to do so or to lie to yourself. Not honoring this fascination, this car crash of desire, is also a lie. So what do you do? Pursue it? Deny it? It doesn't matter. The consequences began when you opened the door and saw the tiger, called it by its name: love. Pursue it or don't, you're already stuck between two truths, two opportunities to lie.

The question is not, as we've always been asked, the lady—beautiful, virtuous, and almost everything we want—or the tiger—passionate, wild, and almost everything we want. The question is, what do we do with our feelings for the lady *and* the tiger. The lady is fair, is home, is delight. The tiger is not bloodthirsty, as we always believed, but, say, romantic. Impetuous. Sharing almost nothing in common with the lady. They even have a different number of feet. But the lady would not see it this way. You already know that.

You can tell the second love that you can't do this—banish the tiger from your life. You can go home to the first, confess your desire, sob on her shoulder, tell her how awful you feel, and she (or he) will soothe you. Until later, when she wonders if you look at all the other zoo animals that way, and every day for a while, if not longer, she will sniff at you to see if you've been near the large cat cages. Things will not be the same for a long time. And you've lost the tiger. Every time the housecat sits on your lap, you tear up thinking of what might have been, the love that has been lost. Your first love asks you what's wrong and you say "nothing." You say nothing a lot, because there's nothing left, nothing inside.

think

- Is the writer's set of options in the final paragraph realistic? Fanciful? Are there, in your opinion, more or fewer options?
- How useful does it seem to you to anticipate and plan for the possibility (or likelihood) of romantic love outside your marriage?
- Does such planning strike you as a safeguard against or a first step toward an actual affair? Why?
- If there's something to the writer's premise that "we have more than one true love after all," what does this imply for the management of your marriage?

think (continued)

pray

read   not for the faint of heart

From *The Wizard of Id* daily comic, by Brant Parker and Johnny Hart[6]

Elderly couple to king: "We've been married 60 years."

King: "What did you do to celebrate?"

Couple: "We burned the prenup agreement."

From "A Twenty-First-Century Ritual," by Erica Jong[7]

The matter of the prenup seemed like very small potatoes compared to what I had discovered. If you join your life with someone's, you become a hostage to fortune in a way that no legal document can protect you against. Marriage is primal stuff—two people confronting their own mortality. It is not for the faint of heart. It is not for beginners.

think

- To a lot of people on the verge of a wedding, a prenuptial agreement is a wise first step in anticipating the unfortunate directions a marriage could go. Theoretically and personally, what do you feel about prenups and what they do or don't do for a marriage?
- In your own words, what did Jong discover about her prenup?
- Have you in your marriage ever felt like "a hostage to fortune"? Describe the circumstances.
- How do you go about planning deliberately for such "primal stuff" as a marriage?

think (continued)

pray

LIVE

what i want to discuss

What have you discovered this week that you definitely want to discuss with your small group? Write that here. Then begin your small-group discussion with these thoughts.

so what?

Use the following space to summarize what you've discovered during this chapter about anticipating decisions in your marriage rather than being caught off guard by life's unpredictable twists and turns. Review your Beginning Place if you need to remember where you began. How does God's truth impact the next step in your journey?

then what?

What is one practical thing you can do to apply what you've discovered? Describe how you will put this into practice. What steps will you take? Remember to think realistically; an admirable but unreachable goal is as good as no goal. Discuss your goal with your small group to further define it.

how?

Identify how you will be held accountable to the goal you described. Who will be on your support team? What are their responsibilities? How will you measure the success of your plan? Write the details here.

outright disagreements

"How do we set goals and make decisions
when we just don't see eye to eye?"

the beginning place

A great marriage is not when the "perfect couple" comes together.
It is when an imperfect couple learns to enjoy their differences.
—David Meurer

One commonly hears three schools of thought and practice on this slice
of married life:

- The most under-advertised aspect of marriage, disagreement is
  inevitable even in the best of partnerships. So just get used to
  living with it.
- Disagreement gradually erodes any relationship, especially
  marriage. So do whatever therapy or reading or communicating or compromising you need to do to eliminate it.
- Disagreement is a boon to a marriage, albeit an unwelcome
  and messy boon. Just as conflict creates a story's plot, so conflict keeps a marriage alert and on the growing edge.

Of course, the truth is nuanced and noodled through *all* of these. What keeps things so variable, what makes different marriages respond differently to spousal disagreements, are things like how each person is wired, the depth of commitment to the marriage, and the frequency and subjects of disagreements.

If you have any doubt about this, just go to Sacred Writ for all sorts of marital disagreements and notice the results of the spats, especially the effects on the couples' further planning and decision-making abilities. Consider a significant disagreement between the matriarch and patriarch Sarah and Abraham (see Genesis chapters 16 and 21), the one about producing an heir. Sarah finally swallowed her pride and determined that their child would be conceived and birthed by her servant Hagar. Abraham acquiesced. Twice Sarah's resentment flared, and she wanted Hagar booted out of the household. Abraham acquiesced again, then again. All this acquiescing by Abraham probably dissolved any disagreement he may have had with his wife and her plans; but by the time you've read to the end of Genesis, you have the feeling that in the long run, the patriarch's acquiescence royally complicated their lives.

Flip a hundred pages or so further and you will read of David and Michal's disagreement about what constituted appropriate public behavior for him (see 2 Samuel 6). The Chest of God (the ark of the covenant, in traditional jargon) was returning to Israel after a long absence, and in the celebration, King David danced "with great abandon"—in Michal's accusative words, "exposing himself to the eyes of the servants' maids like some burlesque street dancer." Ouch. David brushed off not only the criticism but also the wife that spoke it. Their disagreement seems to have killed all marital planning, including, apparently, family planning, for the Bible's last word on Michal is that she was barren the rest of her life.

Then, of course, there was Mary and Joseph's disagreement regarding what to do about her first and most spectacular pregnancy (see Matthew 1). Upon hearing the discomfiting news, Joseph decided to back out of the engagement; we can assume that Mary disagreed with his decision to terminate their engagement, although her defense was hardly convincing. Their presumed disagreement was resolved only by divine intervention, and they went on to plan another day.

Disagreement between spouses in the Bible was just like disagreement between spouses today: They were, and are, resolved and unresolved, violent and icily polite, springing from differing worldviews and different cultures.

So when do outright disagreements get in the way of mutual decision making and deliberate planning in your marriage? Do your attempts at intentionality take the lid off unresolved, back-burner, simmering disagreement? What kinds of disagreement are chronic, and what kinds have blindsided you recently? How do the two of you get through it so that you can make sound decisions? Use the space below to summarize your beginning place for this lesson. Describe those aspects of marital planning where outright disagreement has significantly hindered your forward progress as a couple. We'll start here and then go deeper.

read   hey, i thought *i* was in charge here!

From "Act III, Scene ii," in *The Weather of the Heart: Poems by Madeleine L'Engle*[1]

Someone has altered the script.

My lines have been changed.

The other actors are shifting roles.

They don't come on when they're expected to,

and they don't say the lines I've written

and I'm being upstaged.

I thought I was writing this play

with a rather nice role for myself,

small, but juicy

and some excellent lines.

But nobody gives me my cues

and the scenery has been replaced.

I don't recognize the new sets.

This isn't the script I was writing.

I don't understand this plot at all.

To grow up

is to find

the small part you are playing

in this extraordinary drama

written by

somebody else.

think

- What line or lines in this poem most reflect your feelings about being married? Why?
- To what extent are you writing the "extraordinary drama" of your marriage? To what extent is your spouse writing it? To what extent is God writing it?
- When was the last time you felt upstaged in making what you thought were good, solid plans in your marriage? Talk about that.

think (continued)

pray

read   you *will* fight with your soul mate — so choose your battles carefully

From "Rules of Engagement," by Sandra G. Boodman[2]

One of the first things many premarital therapists do is to explode persistent myths that help sabotage marriages: that love is the most important predictor of marital happiness; that shared interests are a bulwark against divorce; and that true soul mates don't fight.

All are false, researchers have found.

"That's why people feel so set up," said Diane Sollee, founder of Smart Marriages, a marriage education clearinghouse based in the District. She notes that psychologists have found that all couples disagree about the same amount—it's the way they manage conflict that distinguishes satisfied partners from miserable ones.

Unhappy couples and those who divorce tend to resort to what John Gottman, a Seattle psychologist and one of the pioneers of the study of marital behavior, calls "the Four Horsemen of the Apocalypse": criticism, contempt, defensiveness and stonewalling. They get stuck in negative, destructive patterns, have fewer positive interactions than happy couples and are unable to resolve problems.

Linda Peterson Rogers, a marital therapist who practices in Falls Church [Virginia], said one of her goals in premarital counseling is to teach couples acceptance and a recognition that personality characteristics—such as a tendency to be disorganized or late—probably won't change after marriage.

[Social worker Rob] Scuka said he tells couples that if they can't come to a satisfactory resolution, each partner has to decide how important the issue is. Chronic lateness may not be something worth breaking up over; chronic debt might be.

"Couples can and do have very great differences, but the key is a spirit of mutual accommodation," said Scuka. "The problem comes when it's clear one person's primary agenda is getting their needs met."

think

- Which of the observations made in this article about marital disagreements do you experience most often in your own marriage? Least often?
- Put "the Four Horsemen"—criticism, contempt, defensiveness, and stonewalling—in the order in which you typically use them.
- Now order them according to how you perceive your spouse to use them.
- Do you feel it is *ever* appropriate for your primary agenda to be getting your needs met? Why do you feel that way? How could that create a problem in a marriage?

pray

read   money, money, money

From *Toward Commitment: A Dialogue about Marriage*, by Diane Rehm and John B. Rehm[3]

> In the early years of our marriage, the issue of who would control the money arose between us. In my family, it was my mother who wrote the checks, paid the bills, and saved what she could. My father did not seem to object. His very passivity may have strengthened my resolve to be in charge of the money, both before and after our marriage. Even though Diane and I had a joint checking account, I wrote all the checks until one day Diane demanded that she write the checks covering her own needs. I can still recall how shaken and enraged I was by her demand. I can remember attempting to punish her by withdrawing from her for some time. Her presumptuousness seemed to undermine my preeminence as head of the household, including breadwinner and controller. It took me some time to relent and grudgingly accept Diane in this new role.

From *Married: A Fine Predicament*, by Anne Roiphe[4]

> In my second marriage we have often had trouble over money. My mate grew up during the terrible depression of the 1930s and he is frugal and cautious. I am ever hopeful that more money will come from somewhere. Neither of us is very good at real financial investments or plans. We balance each other out. His unrealistic caution tempers my absurd optimism. My optimism tempers his caution. And sometimes we make bad mistakes together for which we try not to blame each other. But at times when tuition bills have been high and extra strains are placed on our budget there is a tension between us that might erupt into something really bad if we aren't very careful.

think

- Recall the details of your first marital disagreement about financial plans and goals. What degree of resolution was achieved?
- What money decisions have you and your spouse made that you only grudgingly accepted? Decisions that your spouse only grudgingly accepted?
- Do the weaknesses of the two of you actually balance out each other in financial ways? Talk about this.

pray

read   just say what's true

James 5:12

> And since you know that [God] cares, let your language show it.
> Don't add words like "I swear to God" to your own words. Don't
> show your impatience by concocting oaths to hurry up God. Just
> say yes or no. Just say what is true. That way, your language can't
> be used against you.

think

- "Just say yes or no. Just say what is true." How, if at all, could
  this apply to your marital disagreements?
- In the middle of a disagreement with your spouse, have you
  been known to advocate a sound decision but use language or
  a verbal manner that only alienates your spouse and turns him
  or her against your plans?
- Where, in your opinion, is there room for compromise, for
  give and take, if for every decision you just say yes or no?

think (continued)

pray

read   talk, stew, or pass?

From *Husbands and Wives: God's Design for the Family*[5]

Select one of the following verbal expressions as an example of the way you responded to a recent conflict in your marriage:

- "It's not important enough to bring up and risk ruining our relationship, so I'll forget it."
- "There's no way to resolve this conflict, so why try?"
- "Let's talk about it. Christ can help us resolve our conflict."
- "Some day I may say something about it, but today I'll just wait and see if it might resolve itself. There are other things we can talk about."

think

- Does this list include your usual reaction in a typical disagreement in your marriage? If so, which is it? If not, what reaction would you add to this list?
- Which of these reactions to marital conflict do you virtually *never* use? Why not?
- This list contains an obvious preferred answer. Do you agree with the writer about that preference? Why or why not? If not, how would you tweak it?

think (continued)

pray

read   church wins big at blackjack

From "Three Marriages: Mrs. Ruth Luger to Mrs. Joanne Lienenkranz," by Garrison Keillor[6]

Dear Joanie,

This is being written Monday night outside of Bakersfield somewhere, a nice motel but right on the highway and the truck traffic sounds like the Russian army. Bob says to say hello. . . .

We saw Bob's cousins Denny and Donny, they live outside Las Vegas where they race cars on weekends at a racetrack and the rest of the time I think they drink beer and say, "Hey, all right." . . .

After dinner it was midnight and Bob and I went to go look at Las Vegas which, just as they say, it never stops, and 4:00 a.m. is the same to them as 4:00 p.m. I know because we stayed up until 4:00 a.m. gambling at the San Remo. Farmers are milking cows now, I thought, and I am playing cards and winning money. In fact, I am getting more money than they earn in a week. Bob wanted to go see Lola Mazola or somebody, some dancer, I said go ahead enjoy yourself. I was hot. I played Blackjack which was the only game I knew how to play (they didn't have Hearts or Rook, ha ha) and I went along pretty well, Bob hanging around and offering dumb advice, and then about 3:30 I had a great feeling and put everything on the table, a bucket of chips, and he almost got a heart attack right there. I won $4,864. Bob was out of the room at the time, sulking in the bar. I cashed in my chips and went and sat down in the booth with him and had a rum and Coke. He just about went crazy when I told him I won and he wanted to know how much. I wouldn't say. A lot. Well, then he wanted some of that to play with and I said no. I said I had promised that it was going to the church. He didn't believe me but I was telling the truth, but he said it was his money to start with. He said, you don't earn no salary. Those were his exact words, spoken to his wife who keeps his house clean and raises up his children. "You don't earn no salary." It was the wrong thing to say to me at that time of the morning. I sailed out through the lobby and down the street. He said he didn't care if I left because he knew I'd come right back but he was walking along behind me as he said it. I walked six blocks in a cold fury with him trotting along behind. I got on a bus, he got on, too, and we rode to the end of the line, out in a regular neighborhood with churches and a school and ranch houses with green lawns and gardens. We walked all the way back as the sun came up and had breakfast at a nice place and slept all day and drove last night and here we are.

The money is in my makeup bag wrapped up in a scarf. Bob says, "That'd completely pay for this trip and leave us plenty for the next trip and then some. It's good luck, we're supposed to enjoy it, not give it away. It's for us, it's like a big wave that comes and lifts us up and off we go to bigger and better things. It could change our whole marriage." He says to me, "Did you promise to God that it'd all go to the church or did you only promise yourself?" To him there's a big difference.

God must've set this trip up so I could learn something. He sure didn't intend it to be fun because it isn't. I found out that I love my husband but I don't really like him very much right now but I'm sticking with him. You look at Sharon and Luanne and you see what happens to people whose word doesn't matter, their lives are a mess. I don't like Bob because he's so weak I think he'd even steal money out of my makeup kit so when he goes to sleep tonight I'll sew it into my dress, forty crisp new hundred-dollar bills, and carry it home and slip it into the collection plate. That'll be nice. Tomorrow we see the zoo and visit one last long-lost friend and then back home to our own house. I hope the kids are behaving themselves.

Love,
your sister Ruth

think

- "I found out that I love my husband," Ruth wrote, "but I don't really like him very much right now but I'm sticking with him." What was the topic of a recent decision in your marriage that made you feel similarly?
- Ruth's decision about how to use her winnings was hardly a shared one — it was more of a personal conviction. Yet what marital agreement could Bob and Ruth have earlier come to that would have covered this specific episode in Las Vegas?
- When it comes to marital decisions and plans, are there some personal nonnegotiables between you and God that you simply aren't willing to compromise on with your spouse? If so, name one or two. If not, why not?

pray

LIVE

what i want to discuss

What have you discovered this week that you definitely want to discuss with your small group? Write that here. Then begin your small-group discussion with these thoughts.

so what?

Use the following space to summarize what you've discovered during this chapter about dealing with outright disagreements with your spouse regarding plans and goals in your marriage. Review your Beginning Place if you need to remember where you began. How does God's truth impact the next step in your journey?

then what?

What is one practical thing you can do to apply what you've discovered? Describe how you will put this into practice. What steps will you take? Remember to think realistically; an admirable but unreachable goal is as good as no goal. Discuss your goal with your small group to further define it.

how?

Identify how you will be held accountable to the goal you described. Who will be on your support team? What are their responsibilities? How will you measure the success of your plan? Write the details here.

mixed marriages

"Just once I'd like to see a marriage between very different people who have figured out how to share the planning and management and goal setting in their relationship."

the beginning place

Nearly all marriages, even happy ones, are mistakes: in the sense that almost certainly (in a more perfect world, or even with a little more care in this very imperfect one) both partners might be found more suitable mates. But the real soul-mate is the one you are actually married to.

—J. R. R. Tolkien, Letter to Michael Tolkien, March 1941

How can two individuals be so intensely attracted to each other only to discover, weeks or years later, how different from each other they are?

It seems a cosmic joke at times. Other times it feels like no joke at all (you don't recall jokes being so *painful*.) but more like God using your sandpapery spouse to grind off your rough edges. And then there's the sociobiology of it all—how we seem hardwired to detect and marry familiarity (i.e., someone like Mom or Dad).

The theology of it, however, is what intrigues most Christian couples. Just what hand does God have in bringing such different persons together and then expecting such a deep degree of partnership between them?

Well, there's the Handpicked By God Just For You theory, in which God creates a person customized for marriage to you. Your duty is to seek God, trust him to lead you to The One, and try not to screw things up.

Then there's the It's Your Choice And God Is Happy With That interpretation, which posits that there are any number of people in this wide world with whom you could be happy, fulfilled, and within God's will. Your responsibility is to choose wisely—and try not to screw things up.

It probably doesn't matter where on this theological spectrum you land, at least when push comes to shove—which is to say when (1) you really want to be happily married to your partner, or (2) you really want out of your marriage. If you want a happy marriage to the one you're with, it hardly matters if the Almighty handpicked your spouse for you or if you did your own choosing. And if you really want out of your marriage—well, let's just say that especially under duress, theology has a way of conforming to one's comfort level. Christians who are determined to change churches or spouses usually find a biblical explanation for it.

Yet many couples stubbornly hold on to their marriage, if not each other, or hold on to their marriage in the hopes of holding each other. They work out the details, raise their children, spot each other in tight situations, try to sidestep the temptations of other intimacies. They manage their marriages. They are intentional and deliberate. They have a long view of marriage. They know that if they let their differences call the shots, there will be pain, then sundering, then a greater or lesser healing. Yet they opt for letting their shared hopes, not their differences, call the shots.

How *any* couple manages to grow on their differences, rather than let their differences define their marriage, is something of a miracle. Yet such mixed marriages that work will cross your path, regularly if not frequently, in a book or article if not in person. Grab those moments, those lives, those models—season your own marriage with them, as much as you can.

So in what way is your marriage mixed—and what does that say about how you and your spouse are able (or unable) to strategize your marriage, to be intentional and deliberate in the planning of your marriage? In what situations have you let your differences enhance your marriage? In what situations are your differences getting in the way of marital planning? Use the space below to summarize your beginning place for this lesson. We'll start here and then go deeper.

read   you're just with who you're with

Anne Tyler, quoted in "Sunbeams," *The Sun*[1]

I knew couples who had been married almost forever—tending each other's illnesses, dealing with money troubles or the daughter's suicide or the grandson's drug addiction. And I was beginning to suspect that it made no difference whether they'd married the right person. You're just with who you're with. You've signed on with her, put in half a century with her, grown to know her as well as you know yourself, and she's *become* the right person, or the only person. I wish someone had told me that earlier; I'd have hung on then.

think

- Does this writer's insight strike you as a cheap reason for staying married (marriage by default), or as one of the strongest reasons for staying married, or somewhere in between? Talk about this.
- In the context of this passage, do you agree or disagree with the writer that it makes no difference whether one marries the right person? Why?
- Recall a marriage you knew that was undone by a family crisis, and a marriage that was strengthened by such a crisis. How do you explain the different outcomes to similar emotional trauma?

think (continued)

pray

read smitten, jaded, or just realistic?

From "Marrying Out of History," by Nell Casey[2]

I was seated next to a well-known painter at a dinner party the other night. He is in his midsixties and has been married for thirty-eight years. When I asked him what stayed the same, what essential bit made his marriage last, he grasped uncomfortably for the answer. "She's still my best friend," he said and then slightly grimaced at his own corny offering. "We amuse each other. We have a shared interest in our children." His eyes closed and fluttered as he concentrated, searching for meaning. "A long marriage can sometimes feel like life imprisonment," he said, suddenly opening his eyes again. "But love also changes again and again and again over the years. Don't expect that what you have now will be what you have down the road. You won't even recognize why you first fell in love." He shrugged, offering one last possibility, "And some people are just lifers."

I felt torn. I respected the words of an intelligent man who has been married decades longer than me. I tried to weave his weary appreciation into our future, imagining Jesse and me one day feeling the same way. And I also shrugged his words off with the impishness of a teenager. I am impatient with those who resist marriage after having chosen it, who don't endorse it wholeheartedly. Why not *love* love? Why let time wear it down? *That won't happen to us*, I thought.

think

- What in the painter's words gives you the sense that he and his wife are or once were very different kinds of people?
- Whose response connects with you most deeply—the painter's or the writer's? Why?
- Which of the painter's several reasons for the longevity of his marriage most resembles what *you* want to say someday about your marriage? Why?

think (continued)

pray

read   options galore

From an interview with William A. Sabin, author of *The Gregg Reference Manual*[3]

> I'm troubled by the number of people who think there's only one correct way of doing things. It drives them crazy to be told that there are options—that they have to make some decisions, that in many cases they have to exercise judgment and taste. It doesn't trouble me if you and I do not make the same decision in a particular situation, but I'd like to think that our decisions are based on a shared perspective on the various rules of style.

think

- The context of Sabin's words is copyediting—yet how thoroughly can his comments be applied to a marriage between very different people who nevertheless want to agree on some plans and goals for their relationship?
- What breadth of options, what leeway, what restrictions do the two of you feel you have in deliberately planning and managing your marriage?
- Even when you and your spouse disagree about management details in your marriage, what "shared perspective" do you both have of the issues? Or *do* you?

think (continued)

pray

read   how to build a marriage

From *The Second Neurotic's Notebook*, by Mignon McLaughlin[4]

> A successful marriage requires falling in love many times, always with the same person.

1 Corinthians 3:9

> Or, to put it another way, you are God's house. Using the gift God gave me as a good architect, I designed blueprints; Apollos is putting up the walls. Let each carpenter who comes on the job take care to build on the foundation! Remember, there is only one foundation, the one already laid: Jesus Christ. Take particular care in picking out your building materials.

think

- What does McLaughlin indicate are the two requirements for a successful marriage?
- In his letter to the Corinthians, what does the apostle Paul say are the requirements for a sound building—like, say, the edifice of your marriage?
- What about McLaughlin's observations have you found to be valid? Invalid?
- What materials do you suppose St. Paul would suggest you use in the building of your marriage?

think (continued)

pray

read the raging gap

From *The Feminine Journey: Understanding the Biblical Stages of a Woman's Life*, by Cynthia and Robert Hicks[5]

Through the course of raising three children, Bob and I have had many conversations about different situations and concerns regarding our kids. I usually want to discuss the issue over and over again, expressing and processing my feelings. Bob finally reaches a point where he gets frustrated and wants to cut off discussion unless we can talk about solutions. His response is usually, "Well, what do you want *me* to do about it?" That always drives me crazy! My answer is usually a frustrated, "I don't know!" I'm not necessarily looking for an answer, just a response of mutual concern. At that point I walk away, angry because he doesn't appear to share my feelings. Then I feel totally responsible for the problem and resentful that he won't share in the burden.

The raging gap between men and women in the area of emotional expression can leave women feeling very alone. Therefore, in reality, a great deal of our emotional support will inevitably come from other women who share common interests and relational needs. The bonds of homemaking, motherhood, careers, shopping, and mutual troubles are natural for women—although they drive men crazy. Whether the emotions are joy or sorrow, it is difficult for most men to come alongside in the way another woman can. Nor should we expect them to.

think

- Do you feel that the writer describes an emotionally impoverished marriage, a tolerable marriage, or as good as it gets?
- Is the emotional connection between you and your spouse more, less, or about the same as the writer's?
- To what degree do you rely on friends for emotional connection? What does your spouse feel about this?

- What depth or exclusivity of emotional connection between you and your spouse is necessary for you to effectively plan intentionally for your marriage?

pray

read   just his hand, on a loaf of bread

From an interview with Marion Woodman, "Men Are from Earth, and So Are Women"[6]

In that moment I was really choosing whether to go on with the marriage or not. I didn't know what was going to happen. What happened is that he put his hand on a loaf of bread, and there was something exquisite about that hand. Compassion came in, and there was no projection. I saw the hand that had made love to me, the hand that had planted tulips with me, the hand that had been my partner for twenty years of my life, and I thought: *This is the man I love. And this is the person I want to work it out with. This is the person who's got the guts to fight it through and find out what a relationship really is.* The compassion I felt for him in that moment—and the compassion I felt for myself—was profound. From that point on, there was no question about our staying together.

I'm not saying everything was peaches and cream afterward. But when we come to difficulties, we both work hard to solve them.

think

- Does this brief narrative strike you as romantic or realistic? Or _____ ? Why?
- Recall a moment of your own like this—seemingly random, yet it decisively turned you one way or the other.
- "For two people who are very different from each other yet married to each other, there *is* no other way for them to share the intentional management of their marriage than through mystical and inexplicable moments of the heart. Rationality is of little use." How would you respond to someone who said that?

think (continued)

pray

LIVE

what i want to discuss

What have you discovered this week that you definitely want to discuss with your small group? Write that here. Then begin your small-group discussion with these thoughts.

so what?

Use the following space to summarize what you've discovered during this chapter about what marriages look like when couples find a way to be mutually intentional and deliberate in their planning. Review your Beginning Place if you need to remember where you began. How does God's truth impact the next step in your journey?

then what?

What is one practical thing you can do to apply what you've discovered? Describe how you will put this into practice. What steps will you take? Remember to think realistically; an admirable but unreachable goal is as good as no goal. Discuss your goal with your small group to further define it.

how?

Identify how you will be held accountable to the goal you described. Who will be on your support team? What are their responsibilities? How will you measure the success of your plan? Write the details here.

hope for your intentional marriage

Decide where to go from here in your marriage and
how to get there.

a time to review

We come to the final lesson in our *Pedaling Tandem for the Long Haul*
discussion guide. But this is not an ending place. With any luck (and
the prayers of people who care for you), you've been discovering
some truths about your life—particularly, your marriage—and have
seen opportunity for change. Positive change. But no matter what has
brought you to this final lesson, you know that it's only a pause in your
journey.

You may have uncovered behaviors or thoughts that demanded
change. Perhaps you've already changed them. Will the changes stick?
How will you and your spouse continue to take the momentum from
this study into next week, next month, and next year? Use your time in
this lesson not only to review what you discovered but also to determine how you'll stay on track tomorrow.

You'll notice that there's a "Live" section in this lesson matched with each of the previous seven lessons. Use this to note the ongoing plans of you and your spouse. Talk about your plans with small-group members. Commit your plans to prayer. And then do what you say you'll do. As you move forward with a renewed sense of purpose, you'll become more confident learning every day how better to live with your mate for better or for worse—and with the confidence will come, gradually, more success at becoming the couple you both want to become.

read   strategic or spontaneous?

Proverbs 20:18

> Form your purpose by asking for counsel,
>> then carry it out using all the help you can get.

think
- What purposes in your marriage need forming?
- For which of them would your spouse have the best counsel?

pray

LIVE

How does God's truth influence the next step you'll take with your spouse in your marriage journey?

How will you take that next step?

How will you be held accountable?

read   details, details

Ezekiel 43:10

> Son of man, tell the people of Israel all about the Temple. . . . Get
> them to go over the layout. . . . Show them the whole plan of the
> Temple, its ins and outs, the proportions, the regulations, and the
> laws. Draw a picture so they can see the design and meaning and
> live by its design and intent.

think

- What kind of layout, if any, do you have for your marriage?
  What are its proportions and regulations? That is, what things
  does your marriage value, and how are those values reflected?
- Draw a picture, a doodle, a sketch, a diagram—something
  illustrative and nonverbal that shows what aspects of your
  marriage are well planned, and which need better planning.

pray

How does God's truth influence the next step you'll take with your
spouse in your marriage journey?

How will you take that next step?

How will you be held accountable?

read   priorities

Luke 14:28-33

"Is there anyone here who, planning to build a new house, doesn't first sit down and figure the cost so you'll know if you can complete it? If you only get the foundation laid and then run out of money, you're going to look pretty foolish. Everyone passing by will poke fun at you: 'He started something he couldn't finish.'

"Or can you imagine a king going into battle against another king without first deciding whether it is possible with his ten thousand troops to face the twenty thousand troops of the other? And if he decides he can't, won't he send an emissary and work out a truce?

"Simply put, if you're not willing to take what is dearest to you, whether plans or people, and kiss it good-bye, you can't be my disciple."

think

- List the top five priorities in your marriage, and then order them from most to least important.
- Note the two that need the most deliberate, intentional planning. What will have to happen for the two of you to achieve that plan without first running out of steam, out of money, or out of vision?

pray

LIVE

How does God's truth influence the next step you'll take with your spouse in your marriage journey?

How will you take that next step?

How will you be held accountable?

read   clashing models

1 Thessalonians 5:14-15

> Gently encourage the stragglers, and reach out for the exhausted,
> pulling them to their feet. Be patient with each person, attentive
> to individual needs. And be careful that when you get on each
> other's nerves you don't snap at each other. Look for the best in
> each other, and always do your best to bring it out.

think

- What kind of planning with your spouse makes you most
  likely to get on each other's nerves? What makes you get
  snappy with each other?
- What can you do to bring out the best in each other during
  those times?

pray

LIVE

How does God's truth influence the next step you'll take with your
spouse in your marriage journey?

How will you take that next step?

How will you be held accountable?

read   pre-acting

Luke 9:60-62

> Jesus refused. "First things first. Your business is life, not death. And life is urgent: Announce God's kingdom!"
>
> Then another said, "I'm ready to follow you, Master, but first excuse me while I get things straightened out at home."
>
> Jesus said, "No procrastination. No backward looks. You can't put God's kingdom off till tomorrow. Seize the day."

think

- What aspects in the future of your marriage can you anticipate now and spend some time planning for?
- What in your marriage requires no more procrastination, no backward looks, but immediate action today?

pray

LIVE

How does God's truth influence the next step you'll take with your spouse in your marriage journey?

How will you take that next step?

How will you be held accountable?

read   outright disagreements

James 5:12

> And since you know that [God] cares, let your language show it.
> Don't add words like "I swear to God" to your own words. Don't
> show your impatience by concocting oaths to hurry up God. Just
> say yes or no. Just say what is true. That way, your language can't
> be used against you.

think

- What would your spouse say is the most common setting
  when your language shows no love, regardless of what you
  say you're feeling?
- What in your marriage needs a crisp *yes* or *no*, right now,
  instead of a *perhaps* or a *later?*

pray

LIVE

How does God's truth influence the next step you'll take with your
spouse in your marriage journey?

How will you take that next step?

How will you be held accountable?

read   mixed marriages

1 Corinthians 3:9

> Or, to put it another way, you are God's house. Using the gift God gave me as a good architect, I designed blueprints; Apollos is putting up the walls. Let each carpenter who comes on the job take care to build on the foundation! Remember, there is only one foundation, the one already laid: Jesus Christ. Take particular care in picking out your building materials.

think

- List a part of your marriage in which your spouse is so obviously the more gifted one, and another part in which you are the more gifted one.
- How receptive or defensive are each of you to the other when it comes to making plans?

pray

LIVE

How does God's truth influence the next step you'll take with your spouse in your marriage journey?

How will you take that next step?

How will you be held accountable?

notes

lesson 1: strategic or spontaneous?

1. Judith Wallerstein and Sandra Blakeslee, *The Good Marriage: How and Why Love Lasts* (Boston: Houghton Mifflin, 1995), 62.

2. Jack and Cynthia Heald, *Loving Your Wife: Strengthening Your Marriage in a Fallen World* (Colorado Springs, CO: NavPress, 1989), 26-27.

3. Annie Dillard, *Pilgrim at Tinker Creek* copyright 1922 by HarperPerennial, 1974), 201, 203.

4. Excerpts from *Babbitt* by Sinclair Lewis, copyright 1922 by Harcourt, Inc. and renewed 1950 by Sinclair Lewis, reprinted by permission of Harcourt Inc.

lesson 2: details, details

1. Cade Foster, "Neither Revolutionary nor Visionary," review of *What Our Mothers Didn't Tell Us: Why Happiness Eludes the Modern Woman,* by Danielle Crittenden (New York: Simon & Schuster, 1999). Review submitted July 31, 2000, http://www.amazon.com/gp/product/0684859599/ref=dp_return_1/103-2786919-8809438?ie=UTF8&n=283155&s=books.

2. Kevin Leman, *Becoming a Couple of Promise* (Colorado Springs, CO: NavPress, 1999), 84-85. (Warm worm joke told by comedian Burt Mustin on Johnny Carson's *The Tonight Show*.)

3. Judith Wallerstein and Sandra Blakeslee, *The Good Marriage: How and Why Love Lasts* (Boston: Houghton Mifflin, 1995), 68.

4. Anne Roiphe, *Married: A Fine Predicament* (New York: Basic Books, 2002), 66-67.

5. Leman, 112.

lesson 3: priorities

1. "Deal Breakers," from *The Questions to Ask Before You Jump into Bed* by Laurie Seale, copyright © 2005 by Laurie Seale. Used by permission of Perigee Books, an imprint of Penguin Group (USA) Inc.

2. Adapted from Paul Mauchline, "Priorities: Family, Self, Work, Spouse," http://www.artofloving.com.

3. Kevin Leman, *Becoming a Couple of Promise* (Colorado Springs, CO: NavPress, 1999), 42-44.

4. Sandra G. Boodman, "Rules of Engagement," *Washington Post*, February 28, 2006, HE01, http://www.washingtonpost.com/wp-dyn/content/article/2006/02/27/AR2006022701027.html.

lesson 4: clashing models

1. Carol Kent, *Secret Longings of the Heart: Overcoming Deep Disappointment and Unfulfilled Expectations* (Colorado Springs, CO: NavPress, 2003), 109.

2. George Eliot, *Middlemarch* (New York: Penguin, 1871-72, 1994), 477-478.

3. James L. Framo, "Explorations in Marital and Family Therapy," http://inspirationpeek.blogspot.com/2006_05_01_inspirationpeek_archive.html.

4. Diane Rehm and John B. Rehm, *Toward Commitment: A Dialogue about Marriage* (New York: Knopf, 2002), 43.

5. Nell Casey, "Marrying Out of History," in *Why I'm Still Married: Women Write Their Hearts Out on Love, Loss, Sex, and Who Does the Dishes*, ed. Karen Propp and Jean Trounstine (New York: Hudson Street Press, 2006), 268-269.

lesson 5: pre-acting

1. From *Ten Lessons to Transform Your Marriage* by John M. Gottman, Ph.D. and Julie Schwartz Gottman, Ph.D. Joan DeClaire, copyright © 2006 by John M. Gottman, Ph.D. and Joan DeClaire. Used by permission of Crown Publishers, a division of Random House, Inc.

2. Lao Tzu, *The Way of Life: Wisdom of Ancient China*, a translation of *Tao Té Ching*, trans. R. B. Blakney (New York: Mentor, 1955), 62, 113.

3. Judith Wallerstein and Sandra Blakeslee, *The Good Marriage: How and Why Love Lasts* (Boston: Houghton Mifflin, 1995), 274-275.

4. Cynthia Heald, *Loving Your Husband: Building an Intimate Marriage in a Fallen World* (Colorado Springs, CO: NavPress, 1989), 59.

5. "My Cheatin' Heart: When Love Comes Knocking Do You Answer the Door?" by Daphne Gottlieb from *Homewrecker: An Adultery Reader,* copyright 2005, Soft Skull Press, article adapted for Utne. Used by permission of author.

6. Brant Parker and Johnny Hart, *The Wizard of Id* (Creators Syndicate, Inc.), September 7, 2006, http://www.creators.com/comics_show .cfm?next=10&ComicName=wiz. By permission of John L. Hart FLP and Creators Syndicate, Inc.

7. Erica Jong, "A Twenty-First-Century Ritual," in *Why I'm Still Married: Women Write Their Hearts Out on Love, Loss, Sex, and Who Does the Dishes*, ed. Karen Propp and Jean Trounstine (New York: Hudson Street Press, 2006), 79.

lesson 6: outright disagreements

1. "Act III, Scene ii," in *The Weather of the Heart: Poems by Madeleine L'Engle*. Reprinted from *The Weather of the Heart* Copyright © 1978, 2001, by Crosswicks, Ltd. Used by permission of WaterBrook Press, Colorado Springs, CO. All rights reserved.

2. Sandra G. Boodman, "Rules of Engagement," *Washington Post*, February 28, 2006, HE01, http://www.washingtonpost.com/wp-dyn/

content/article/2006/02/27/AR2006022701027.html.

3. Diane Rehm and John B. Rehm, *Toward Commitment: A Dialogue about Marriage* (New York: Knopf, 2002), 72.

4. Anne Roiphe, *Married: A Fine Predicament* (New York: Basic Books, 2002), 18-19.

5. The Navigators, *Husbands and Wives: God's Design for the Family* (Colorado Springs, CO: NavPress, 1980), 49-50.

6. Garrison Keillor, "Three Marriages: Mrs. Ruth Luger to Mrs. Joanne Lienenkranz," *We Are Still Married: Stories and Letters* (New York: Viking, 1989), 83-85.

lesson 7: mixed marriages

1. Anne Tyler, quoted in "Sunbeams," *The Sun*, August 2006, 48.

2. From *Why I'm Still Married* edited by Karen Propp and Jean Trounstine (Hudson Street Press, Penguin Group USA, Inc.). Copyright © 2006 by Nell Casey. Reprinted by permission of Nell Casey.

3. William A. Sabin, author of *The Gregg Reference Manual*, in an interview "on the business of language," upon the release of the book's tenth edition, in *Copy Editor: Language News for the Publishing Professional* 16, no. 3, August–September 2004.

4. Mignon McLaughlin, *The Second Neurotic's Notebook* (Indianapolis: Bobbs-Merrill, 1966), http://www.bookreporter.com/community/quote/01-06.asp.

5. Cynthia and Robert Hicks, *The Feminine Journey: Understanding the Biblical Stages of a Woman's Life* (Colorado Springs, CO: NavPress, 1994), 108-109.

6. Marion Woodman, interview by James Kullander, "Men Are from Earth, and So Are Women," *The Sun*, August 2006, 10.

MORE FROM THE REAL LIFE STUFF FOR COUPLES SERIES.

Shooting the Rapids in a Wooden Canoe
The Navigators
ISBN-13: 978-1-60006-164-6
ISBN-10: 1-60006-164-8

While many people enjoy surprises, no one is thrilled with change. And no marriage, no matter how insulated, is immune to unexpected changes. This study provides couples with a solid road map for anticipating new developments, such as having children and caring for aging parents.

Running a Three-Legged Race Across Time
The Navigators
ISBN-13: 978-1-60006-018-2
ISBN-10: 1-60006-018-8

In one word, describe your marriage. If you answered anything other than "perfect," you need the honest truth from this new Bible discussion guide on staying married in a culture hostile to marriage.

Dancing the Tango in an Earthquake
The Navigators
ISBN-13: 978-1-60006-019-9
ISBN-10: 1-60006-019-6

Together with your spouse or a couples small group, read excerpts about seven major marriage distractions and how you can prevent them from clouding your view of the ultimate prize: a marriage that works.

To order copies, visit your local Christian bookstore, call NavPress at 1-800-366-7788, or log on to www.navpress.com.

To locate a Christian bookstore near you, call 1-800-991-7747.

NAVPRESS®
BRINGING TRUTH TO LIFE
www.navpress.com